The Logical Book

A SUPERTRAMP

Compendium

Laura Shenton

The Logical Book

A SUPERTRAMP

Compendium

Laura Shenton

WP
WYMER
PUBLISHING
Bedford, England

First published in Great Britain in 2020
by Wymer Publishing
www.wymerpublishing.co.uk
Tel: 01234 326691
Wymer Publishing is a trading name of Wymer (UK) Ltd

ISBN: 978-1-912782-36-9

Edited by Jerry Bloom
Typeset and Design by 1016 Sarpsborg
Printed by Imago Group.

A catalogue record for this book is available from the British Library.

"The music always came pretty easily. Both the music and the lyrics come from the same place. For me, composing is literally losing myself in the music. I let the inspiration just come naturally. It is a very magical process. When I start hearing melodies, then I just start singing and the words start coming. The words will have something to do with what I am going through in my life, or what's in my heart at the time. I will have an idea of what the song's about and then work with the melody."
Roger Hodgson

CONTENTS

Foreword

"Laura Shenton has a great passion for the music of Supertramp,
and it shows in "The Logical Book."
It's a no-nonsense collation of the group's interviews and reviews,
amid her incisive comments. The emphasis is almost exclusively
on writing, recording and performing the music. The book gives
valuable insight into Supertramp's oeuvre."

John Helliwell

SUPERTRAMP

PERFORM

"CRIME·OF THE CENTURY"

FIRST AMERICAN TOUR!

APRIL 4
Uptown Theatre, Milwaukee, Wisconsin
APRIL 6
Sports Centre, University of Montreal, Canada
APRIL 7
Convention Center, Quebec City, Canada
APRIL 9
Ottawa Tech High School, Ottawa, Canada
APRIL 11
Beacon Theatre, New York City, N.Y.
APRIL 12
Orpheum, Boston, Mass.
APRIL 13
Gaston Hall, Georgetown Univ., Washington, D.C.

APRIL 14
Earlinger Theatre, Philadelphia, Penn.
APRIL 15
Ford Auditorium, Detroit, Michigan
APRIL 17
Massey Hall, Toronto, Canada
APRIL 18
Kleinhaus Auditorium, Buffalo, New York
APRIL 19
Allen Theatre, Cleveland, Ohio
APRIL 20
Riviera Theatre, Chicago, Illinois
APRIL 25
Sanata Monica Civic Auditorium, Las Angeles, CA

ALSO APPEARING: CHRIS DE BURGH

A&M RECORDS

(More dates to be announced)

Preface

Supertramp! What an amazing band! I trust that you will share such bias with me in reading this book. There is so much to say about them in terms of their unique contribution to music. The last book that was written about the band was published in 1986 and is now out of print.

On such basis, the time feels right to offer an objective insight into Supertramp, their music and the fascinating journey of the band; there were so many highs and lows worth documenting, from the band being funded by a millionaire, to the funding being withdrawn, to the band having their first commercial breakthrough in 1974 with *Crime Of The Century* to exceeding their own expectations with the colossal success of *Breakfast In America* in 1979.

In the interests of transparency and context, as author of this book I have no affiliation with Supertramp and I have no affiliation with any of the band's associates. I was born in 1988, so quite a while after most of the band's most prominent achievements. As a result of this, the content of this book is derived from extensive research fuelled by a passion for Supertramp's amazing music as well as the hoarding of a range of vintage articles.

On the basis of the later, if you're looking for a biography that's full of gossip and intensely detailed information on the personal lives of the band members, you won't find that here. Ultimately, that is not information for me to give and inevitably I don't have it anyway. What I do have though is an abundance of research on Supertramp and it certainly feels right to collate that here in order to offer an angle on the music and achievements of a band whose musical legacy certainly warrants such exploration.

And of course, this book will provide comment on the solo projects of the key members; that feels really important to do because in many cases, a musician's work as a solo artist can often be demonstrative of their propensity to contribute to a group effort or at least, certainly an insight into their musical interests as individuals.

I have tried to keep speculation and rumours down to an absolute minimum. Whilst I may add my own opinion here and there in the name of being objective, essentially I feel that it is important to refer to fact as much as possible throughout my telling of the Supertramp story. As a result, you're going to see a lot of quotes from vintage interviews in this book. I think that's important because there's probably going to come a time where stuff like that gets harder and harder to find. It needs to be collated because Supertramp's contribution to music is certainly worthy of such archiving and indeed, discussion.

Chapter One:
Introducing Supertramp

The band that came to be known as Supertramp started off as a band called Daddy. That was their name from 1969 to 1970. They were formed in London in 1969 and whilst they have often been categorised under the heading of progressive rock, it is certainly the case that they are just as recognisable under rock, pop and indeed art rock. Call their music what you like but there is no denying that it is brilliant. Of course, you're probably biased in reading this book. Bloody well right!

Prominent use of the Wurlitzer electric piano and saxophone have often been a distinctive feature in Supertramp's music. Whilst their earlier style was more progressive, the commercial success came when more radio friendly pop elements were embraced in the mid seventies. By then, the band had sold more than sixty million albums.

That was just the tip of the iceberg though; the classic (and by many people's consideration, most monumental of the band's albums), *Breakfast In America* sold more than twenty million copies. Supertramp were (and arguably still are) absolutely massive in Canada; two of the albums, *Crime Of The Century* and *Breakfast In America* were diamond certified there. That's literally the equivalent of going platinum ten times over for each album! What an achievement and then some!

It was reported in *Cash Box* in June 1980; "Supertramp has sold so many records in Canada that the Canadian Recording Industry Association (CRIA) came up with the new Diamond Award, equivalent to ten platinum LPs. To mark the event, A&M Canada executives flew to Los Angeles to present the awards to the group and its manager, Dave Margereson."

The event was also reported in *Record World* in the same month. Roger Hodgson was quoted in the *Chronicle Herald* in November 2006; "*Crime Of The Century* went to number one in England first, but it took off in Canada shortly after. America took much longer, Canada discovered us very early on and it spread like wildfire. It started in Quebec, but it soon became this huge love affair with Canada, it was pretty phenomenal."

Oh and Canada, the feeling seems to be mutual, as Hodgson was quoted in the Canadian paper, *The Standard* in December 2008; "I've always felt very at home in Canada. Obviously it is where Supertramp first broke in North America in the seventies and there's been a love affair ever since. I'm overjoyed to feel so welcomed back and feel the renewed affection for my songs that seem to have been such a backdrop for so many Canadians' lives. I remember they told me one in twenty Canadians owned *Crime Of The Century* and *Breakfast In America*. And now just recently, my DVD, *Take The Long Way Home* went double platinum in Canada within months, which touched me very much."

Summer 1973 was a pivotal time in the band's history. Not commercially, they were still pretty small time then. But from a personnel perspective, things were in a state of dilemma. The band's founders, Rick Davies and Roger Hodgson had reached a point where, after two albums (*Supertramp* and *Indelibly Stamped*) with two different line-ups, they had achieved critical acclaim for the music itself. Davies and Hodgson were on the fence about whether to call it a day or to begin the search for new musicians. Having decided to give it one more go, after what seemed like an endless flurry of auditions, they finally recruited Dougie Thomson, a bassist from Glasgow, who had played with the Alan Bown Set; John Anthony Helliwell, a saxophonist from Yorkshire (also from the Alan Bown Set) and Bob Siebenberg, a Californian drummer who had been playing pub rock with the band, Bees Make Honey. This was ultimately the magic combination of personnel that would be instrumental in getting the ball rolling again for Supertramp.

The band set up house together in later 1973; a little cottage in Southcombe in Somerset. It was there that Rick and Roger began writing the songs that would eventually become key material for the *Crime Of The Century* album. With rehearsals having gone well, the band agreed that it was time to enlist the help of producer Ken Scott who had worked with David Bowie and Mahavishnu Orchestra. They were clearly pleased to have him on board. As Helliwell was quoted in *Sounds* in May 1976, "He was right for us. He taught us all about the studio. He doesn't play anything which is good because if he did it might be a too many cooks type of thing. His instrument is the desk and sounds."

The album was recorded at Trident Studios in London. *Crime Of The Century* was released in 1974 and became a rock classic. Evidently, Supertramp had found their formula and they were on their way to what would become even greater musical and commercial highs. As with all things worth doing though, it was never plain sailing for the band — that would be too easy. In 1979 there was quite the balls up made when a show in Paris only sold eight tickets (six of which the promoter had purchased himself!).

Equally though, the band played four sold out shows there to thousands of people each night. A small blip in a history of predominantly massive achievements I suppose. *Crime Of The Century* had certainly won over audiences on a large scale whereby the album reached number one in the UK and with an overall successful European tour behind them, Supertramp were at the point where it was time to see if they could crack America. It worked. The band were awarded what was to be their first of many gold LPs.

The next album, *Crisis? What Crisis?* Was recorded at A&M Studios in Los Angeles. There was a bit of a delay in the process though; the band had to wait while Roger was recovering from a broken arm. He had sustained the injury on the American part of the *Crime Of The Century* tour. This resulted in the *Crisis? What Crisis?* album needing to be finished at Scorpio Studios in London.

Crisis? What Crisis? was released in the autumn of 1975 and once again it was time for a world tour. Having become more high profile by this point, a much larger stage production was part of the show; It incorporated extensive lighting, sound and films and a team of technicians that was affectionately named the Supertramp Army. The ambitious tour ran for eight months. Supertramp was a tremendously big deal by this point. Even *The Sun* newspaper decided to put them on page three, the iconic page of *The Sun* that was typically reserved for (for want of better term) topless women. Still though, the essence of page three was kept intact; a scantily dressed woman was draped across the laps of the band members.

After a show at the Royal Albert Hall, it was time for Supertramp to go back to America. The American and Canadian tours that followed were elaborate; they saw the band play to both major and small scale venues as well as Las Vegas, which wasn't common for a band of their stature at the time. The tour just kept on going! The next stop was Japan, followed by Australia and New Zealand. It was by the autumn of 1976 that Supertramp had moved to live in California. They also chose an interesting location from which to work on their next album; Caribou Ranch, in the snowy mountains of Colorado.

After three months at Caribou, the band returned to Los Angeles with engineers Geoff Emerick and Pete Henderson to mix the album at the Record Plant. The crew had to go back to Caribou though; they had to drag a grand piano up a mountain top to photograph the cover for the album, *Even In The Quietest Moments...* Oh, and this was all during a snowstorm. Must have been outrageously difficult! Suffering in the name of art and all that!

Yet again, another tour was undertaken. It covered one hundred and thirty cities in America, Canada, Europe and England. Touring had become a way of life for Supertramp and the band embraced the opportunity to throw some humour into the mix, a seemingly sensible decision when working so hard. John began to wear funny costumes on stage, one of which featured Spiderman glasses. It seemed at this stage the band were at the peak of their game as they were welcomed to Wembley Arena for the UK part of their tour but no, there was still much more to come. *Breakfast In America*.

The album cover is of Libby, the big and bubbly waitress, posing excitedly in front of the Statue of Liberty, holding a glass of orange juice against the Manhattan skyline. Hodgson was quoted in *Classic Rock Revisited* in February 2012; "We were very involved with the sleeve. We had a guy named Mike Dowd that we had worked with for a couple of covers. We gave him our ideas and he came to us with his ideas. Eventually, he came to us with the idea in sketch form. I remember choosing the lady that was on the cover, her name was Libby. The original cover had a sexy, young waitress but we felt that wasn't us. We felt like a more frumpy, twinkly, middle aged lady would be better. We chose the lady from a modelling agency. It really represented the more eccentric quality of the band. It was a great idea."

The model's name was actress Kate Murtagh and she got to go to lots of events with the band as they celebrated the success of *Breakfast In America*. In April 1979, *Cash Box* reported; "Supertramp introduced its *Breakfast In America* cover girl, Libby, to members of A&M's Japanese affiliate, Alfa Records, backstage following their recent Forum concert. The band plans to tour the Far East in the late fall."

Supertramp's 1979 album was (and still is) iconic. Inevitable really considering the extent to which it had global success when it came out. The theme of the album was based on the band's experiences of being British and swarmed in American culture. The album went to number one in virtually every country in the world. It simply kept on climbing. It surpassed gold and went platinum, sales had eventually reached sixteen million by 1980. The album was absolutely massive. When Supertramp celebrated the album going platinum, Holland awarded them with plexiglass-enclosed trays of each band members favourite breakfast. Such a lovely reward considering that the band had never really anticipated such a large scale of success. So much so that Rick Davies had bet Bob Siebenberg one hundred dollars that the album wouldn't reach the top five in the American charts. The joys of being wrong sometimes!

Davies paid Siebenberg the money at a party after a sold-out show in New York's Madison Square Garden where A&M records awarded the band their first of many platinum awards. *Breakfast In America* stayed in the American top five for twenty two weeks. A big album justified a big tour. As such, the tour for the album consisted of five million dollars worth of equipment. This included fifty-two tonnes of equipment, ten miles of cable, and a forty-man crew. The tour definitely paid for itself though; it broke all previously set records on concert attendance in Europe and Canada. The whole time was an absolute whirlwind of riding high on the wave of success. They were awarded diamond status in Canada for the sales of *Crime Of The Century* and *Breakfast In America*, had sold the most albums in America in 1979 and had literally walls full of gold and platinum record awards from Europe. Hodgson and Davies were also awarded a gold record for their first Supertramp album. By the end of a ten-month tour, it was time for a well-earned rest.

By late 1981 the priority was to get back in the studio for another album, this time called ...*Famous Last Words*... It was rehearsed in Rick's studio and mostly recorded at Roger's and was released in late 1982. By this time, videos played an important role in promoting music. Like many bands who had arguably had the peak of their success in the seventies, the eighties perhaps left Supertramp feeling disillusioned with the direction in which they were going.

After many meetings on deciding what to do next, things had reached the point where Roger was adamant that he needed to leave in order to work on his solo career. It seems that the feeling was mutual and certainly one from an artistic perspective more than anything else. Rick was also keen to make a success of things and he carried on with the Supertramp name. Perhaps it was the case that the public were predominantly oblivious to what Supertramp were doing by that point. That said, although ticket sales were moving slowly, they still sold out many venues when they toured. Supertramp never really went away.

In a press conference, Princess Diana declared that they were her favourite band. Clearly, Supertramp had reached so many people since they had begun the band in 1969. As was reported in the *Daily Express* on 14th July 1983, "four years ago the Three Degrees all-girl pop group attained royal approval when Prince Charles, their number one fan, invited them to his thirtieth birthday party at Buckingham Palace. Since then Charles, who actually prefers classical music, has shown a predilection for Status Quo and next week he will be taking Princess Diana to a charity concert in London, given by Britain's top group Duran Duran. But in an off-the-cuff answer, the group Diana really prefers is Supertramp. Known as the faceless five because of their quest for anonymity, this British rock group is one of the hottest sounds around. It is perhaps no surprise that Supertramp are the Princess of Wales' favourite. Through their reflective, contemporary rock songs they attracted a massive following of female admirers. By their own choice, little is known of the individuals other than their musical backgrounds. The group is made up of Roger Hodgson from Buckingham (shortly to leave), Richard Davies from Swindon, Dougie Thomson from Glasgow, John Helliwell from Yorkshire and Bob Benberg from California. They have sold more than sixty million albums worldwide. But selling millions is no match for receiving the royal seal of approval."

This is a good point at which to note, that in the public eye, Supertramp has been very much about the band as a whole rather than the personal lives of the group's five members. In such regard, I'll clarify to you now that this book is about the group and their music rather than a tale of personalities, characters or celebrity. Also, the name of Supertramp's drummer is Bob Siebenberg but due to being credited on the band's earlier albums as Bob C. Benberg, he has been referred to as all kinds of variations of his actual name in many articles. In the interest of authenticity, I will transcribe his name as it was originally written so you will see all kinds of variations on his name throughout this book.

As the members of the band have said in numerous interviews that are quoted throughout this book, Supertramp was a nameless band as in, it was about the band as a whole rather than the musicians as individuals. It is very plausible that someone could be a fan of Supertramp and not necessarily able to name all members of the band. They were not household names and this is something that presented as a challenge commercially when they did solo projects. In such regard, comment on the personal lives and details on each band member has been quite minimal in the media and that will therefore be the case throughout this book. Journalist Brian Harrigan, described the band in his *Melody Maker* report in November 1975; "They're quiet spoken, reserved and have, with the exception of reeds man John Helliwell, no stage presence. They recognise this and compensate with an extensive light show and judicious use of curtains, backdrops and similar visuals."

In June 1979, the *Melody Maker* journalist who interviewed Supertramp considered; "Rick Davies and Roger Hodgson rule Supertramp with a velvet fist. Their influence is unobtrusive but firm. There is an unspoken rule that the privacy of the individual must not be infringed. Supertramp is a very exclusive family. In three days with the band, I don't think I saw Davies and Hodgson converse once, other than to exchange courteous greetings. They're very different personalities but they both write interestingly pertinent songs, with a depth of content that's often overlooked in the rush to applaud (or criticise) the delicacy and prettiness of their music."

In such regard, Roger Hodgson was quoted in the same feature; "We have a strange relationship. It's always been a strange one. We're both oddballs and we've never been able to communicate too much on a verbal level. There's a very deep bond, but it's definitely mostly on a musical level. When there's just the two of us playing together, there's an incredible empathy. His down to earth way of writing, which is very rock 'n' roll, balances out my lighter, melodic style. He's never been the easiest guy to communicate with anyway. I know very few people who're able to get through to him. He doesn't open himself up to people at all. He wants to. But he really cares. He cares too much. That's the trouble, he's oversensitive."

Davies said of the emotional element of his song writing as he was quoted in *Melody Maker* in June 1979; "It's just feelings that you have from time to time. The *Crime Of The Century* album certainly had that aspect of cynicism to it. That was a little more calculatedly cynical than perhaps from the heart… It gets to be a very personal thing. I don't think that half of the frustration that I feel sometimes has ever come out as much as it can. Maybe it did on 'Nervous Wreck' but that's not as true as 'Casual Conversations'. That song, for me, is deeply personal. It can obviously relate to people, as well as boy-girl. I suppose it's me and Roger to a degree — me not being able to communicate with him, wanting to get out at times… That's the thing about this group, it does reach a lot of crisis points, but it never quite blows up. The characters never quite get to that point. I guess that's what has kept us together."

Rick was quoted in August 1977 in *New Musical Express*; "We don't have fights but we're not the greatest talkers so we get the slight undercurrents from time to time." Roger was quoted in the same article; "Our policy has always been to try and let everything happen naturally, which sometimes goes overboard. A problem might start off as something very small and not get talked about because we're waiting for it to iron itself out naturally, but it doesn't. So it builds up and builds up, people talk about it and then you have to have a meeting. In the end, it's nothing."

Far be it from me to draw such conclusion, but to consider Supertramp as a band of introverts would perhaps not seem too farfetched. Besides, as Roger was quoted in *Melody Maker* in November 1975, "there's a mellow vibe about the band. I suppose we're all pretty introverted but that's the way it is. It shows in the music — it's simply, well, mellow, I can't think of a better word to describe it."

Supertramp's under-the-radar type relationship with the media has always seemed to be apparent. In *Melody Maker* in June 1979, an interview with the band was introduced as their first in two years. It doesn't actually make it clear if that was a *Melody*

Maker thing or a general thing but either way, that's certainly noteworthy in relation to Supertramp's musical output. I think *Melody Maker* put it best when in January 1975, succinct biographies of the band members from the classic Supertramp line-up were featured.

Bob Benberg's brief biography was written as follows; "Bob is a self-effacing Californian from Glendale who first tried his hand at drumming at the age of twelve, using a kit belonging to the son of his father's boss, who was involved in making tape copies. He borrowed the drums to join 'a little surf band that my brother and his friends were getting together. I went and played with them and it was really fun and everybody liked it. So for Christmas I got a drum set. That band turned into a band called the Expressions and we did all the local dances down Glendale', from there Bob went on through a series of bands — the Lost Souls, the Ilford Subway and Ben Becula — playing around the Sunset Strip and making a record produced by Terry Melcher. 'I'd been planning to come to England for a while just to get out of Los Angeles because I was tired of hitting the same sort of wall, if you didn't know the guys who were working already and who had the good gigs there was no way of getting to know them. I sold my car and stuff to get here and when I got here I looked around and the first ad I rung in the *Melody Maker* turned into Bees Make Honey and I made some good friends there. Playing with the Bees got me round and got me playing. It helped me. About a year or so into the Bees, we did a tour with Frankie Miller and Supertramp and it evolved from there.' Bob's sympathetic style of drumming is what made him an interesting proposition to Supertramp. He has an economical style which lends itself well to the percussive piano playing of Rick Davies. 'I just play the songs the way I hear them and absorb the ideas from Rick and Roger. When their ideas about drumming are better than mine I use them.' Although he is full of praise for the song writing abilities of Davies and Hodgson, Bob is interested in writing himself, 'I've never learned a melody instrument and while we were doing the album, just out of boredom I decided to learn how to play the piano. I've learned it basically so I'm going to try to turn that into making up a few tunes.' However, he is not interested in the more technical side of records such as production, 'I'm happy just playing the drums really. If I think something's got to go this way or that way I throw out my ideas but I'm never so positive about it that I want to be the guy that says 'that's the way it's going to go!' I just don't want to get into that, I want to be a little more sure of what I have to think about before being put in a position like that. I figure if we've got a guy like Ken Scott around we should let him make the decisions. I don't want any part of that really'."

You'll notice readers, that the above biography is all about the person as a musician rather than with regards to personal stuff. Cool. The days when the music press was not about celebrity I suppose. Notably, Bob Siebenberg did get round to doing that solo project that he said he aspired to when quoted by *Melody Maker* in January 1975. In 1985, he released a solo album called *Giants In Our Own Room* where he sang lead vocals on half of the songs and also played keyboards and drums and indeed in 2013 he released another solo album, *Glendale River*. As with all members of Supertramp, there are parts of the Internet that state their dates of birth and family situations but frankly 1) the information is inconsistent and 2) none of the sources are particularly reliable so again, I'm going to stick to what is known with greater certainty whilst enjoying the fact that Supertramp was about the music, like with many bands whose members were of the post World War Two generation.

So of course, onto the mini biography of John Helliwell, as was also featured in *Melody Maker* in January 1975; "John Helliwell is perhaps the most musically talented in Supertramp, from a playing point of view, he plays a wide variety of instruments from Elka String synthi to flute, although he considers himself first and foremost a tenor sax player. He's a very genial person and where Rick Davies has his darker, more sombre moods interspersed between levity, John is almost continually jovial. He admits that one thing that really gets him down is illness — and he's hardly ever ill. Essentially a jazz buff, the bands he likes most are Weather Report and Chick Corea's Return To Forever, tastes which are evident in the rambling, occasionally pyrotechnic tenor sax lines he puts into Supertramp numbers. From recorder and piano lessons at school, John, who comes from Yorkshire, progressed to clarinet in a small symphony orchestra up north and a few local dance bands. He went to Birmingham, following his profession as a computer programmer and 'got caught up with a group called Jugs O'Henry, a kind of blues-type band. At the invitation of the management, who were handling the Moody Blues at the time, we went to London, we were really naïve and broke up after a while so I was left stranded in London. I put an ad in the *Melody Maker* and one of the calls I got was from Alan Bown so I joined up with him and stayed for a long time.' The band split and after an abortive effort with a group called Wizard, John met up with Dougie (Thomson) again, who he had met originally with Alan Bown, and was added to the ranks of Supertramp. In his time John has also worked in the backing bands of such people as Johnny Johnson and Arthur Conley, which perhaps explains his feeling that Supertramp might become a little more funky in the future, 'I sort of slid into rock from jazz and was in the blues thing in Birmingham. I've got a very wide range of stuff that I like. I like soul music still. Some of my favourite singers are soul — people like Aretha Franklin and Donny Hathaway. Then on the other hand I like any good sax player — Sonny Rollins, John Coltrane, Charlie Parker — all the greats really. I like classical as well.' Supertramp is the first band that John has sung seriously in but he doesn't see himself developing this side of his music, 'No, not really. I haven't got such a good voice. I'd like to develop my sax playing a lot more.' On stage, John has his work cut out with the number of instruments he is called on to play. In their current stage show, which lasts for about seventy-five minutes, he has about a minute when he is not playing, 'But I like playing on stage. I'm just a blower really. There's a buzz you get from an audience which is really great'."

And for Dougie Thomson (they spelt his name as Thompson but I've corrected it in my transcription because I don't feel like being pedantic about it), *Melody Maker* offered the following mini biography in January 1975; "Dougie Thomson, a lean and hungry-looking Scotsman from Glasgow, is the third oldest serving member of the band after Davies and Hodgson. He joined the band in Scotland and they took refuge from the pop-orientated music scene there by going to Germany to do the usual half hour on, half hour off work in Frankfurt's clubs. 'A fantastic life — some of the best times I've had playing in bands was then. It was certainly the most carefree. You didn't have the same sort of pressures and responsibilities that you have now. It's very serious now, it's your whole lifestyle. I came back after that and I'd got the music bug even more. I'd given up all hopes of any other sort of career but things in Scotland by this time were getting incredibly stale. There were people like Frankie Miller, Stone The Crows, the Average White Band, who were slowly moving to London so I went with them.' After a "soul destroying" period of plodding around auditions, he moved into a flat with a guy who he'd known in Scotland who had just joined Alan Bown. Their bassist left so Dougie got the gig. In the band at the time was John Helliwell and, after Alan Bown split, he and Dougie did some cabaret work together. Dougie spotted an ad in the *Melody Maker* for a bass player for Supertramp, answered it, and got the job, 'We all found we had the same sort of influences, the same sort of direction so it was really good. But when I joined, the group were really going through a transitional period. Rick and Roger were really developing as writers and their development had outgrown the sort of gig to gig survival basis that the band was in. So we decided to knock it on the head and start all over again from scratch. The sax player then was really good but his heart wasn't in it and the drummer was excellent but he had a very strong personality and the group needs to be co-operative. He was very dominant so that didn't work out really. We were terribly fortunate in finding Bob as a drummer and I knew John knew his personality was right for the band, he joined, and that was it really.' Asked what attracted him originally about Supertramp, he said, 'The songs, no two ways about it. Rick and Roger are the most interesting song writers I've ever come across. The songs fascinated me when I joined the band — there's an incredible variety in it. You're not tied down to one kind of music, every song's another approach.' Dougie says his own style of playing has become more refined since he joined Supertramp, 'I think it's a lot more sympathetic than it ever was before. I play less and less now, just the right places really. I'm more aware of the song, what's right for the song rather than what I feel about playing. Before it was very much a rhythm section thing, getting tight with the drummer and that would be it. Now I'm aware of everything that's going on and trying to play to that.' Dougie is concerned that Rick and Roger should not be "stifled" in any way, 'They really need the freedom to know that if they come up with things the people around them are going to be thinking on the same lines.' Does this mean that he feels dominated by Davies and Hodgson? 'Not in the slightest. Everybody's got a part to play. It's their deal because they're the songwriters but it stops there really. If anyone of us doesn't like what's going on we'll speak up. There's a freer, healthier atmosphere in the group now compared to when I first joined'."

Rick Davies' short biography in *Melody Maker* in January 1975 was; "The man who started Supertramp, Richard Davies, is an ambivalent character. He is recognised as the band's humorist and yet, when the conversation turns to music he is deadly

serious, hardly ever allowing even the ghost of a smile to cross his face. He started out on drums, beginning with lessons for about three years, a stint in the local brass bands back home in Swindon and then into groups. He gradually taught himself to play piano and has remained on that instrument since. Through his interest in blues and boogie and because there was no one he knew who could play, he had to take up piano, 'I built up a little repertoire of chords and what I'm doing now is completely untutored. I don't really know the chords. I just built my own thing up on it, a sort of primitive style.' Rick went to Europe with a band for two weeks and stayed for two years, earning his daily crust through club work. After a series of ups and downs, Rick came back to Britain to form Supertramp, 'There were a lot of good things happening then like Traffic and Spooky Tooth, which was a surprise to me when I came back from the Continent because I was a bit dubious, and then to realise that there were good bands around made me realise Supertramp could work, there was an audience for it.' This sense of being dubious about things is something which persists today for Rick. He said about his songwriting, 'I'm always suspicious of everything I do, really very self critical, that seems to be the only way to go around. You can never be on top of song writing I don't think.' Is he satisfied with Supertramp at the moment? 'You're never really satisfied. It's just that things that were bugging the band a year ago have all gone. Those problems are gone but you find different problems coming out. There are no problems with the actual playing anymore, it's a question of the reason for playing and that sort of thing and actually coming out and not just turning out fodder. As far as the future is concerned, I don't know. I'd like to do a couple of albums maybe with this set-up and maybe if we could get enough people interested, bring some other people in. I don't know. It's a question of keeping fresh really.' Does he consider himself the leader of the band? 'No, I don't think so. The ideal, the absolute ideal, is everybody really having enough to express themselves. The guy who is my real inspiration is Duke Ellington. He wrote for the individual members and brought everything out for them. If somebody left, they'd drop the whole number. I listen to a lot of jazz, which is away from what we're doing but it's all good quality stuff. The only influence of that on our music is the taste. Good jazz is just playing for the music. There's no ego in it at all — the sort of stuff I like anyway — and that's it really, that's the only influence. It's just a very basic thing like taste which you can relate to anything. Controlling ego is the thing. Obviously you need some just to get up on stage but keeping it in perspective is all important'."

Throughout this book, you'll notice that Hodgson and Davies often feature more in the narrative than the other three members of the classic Supertramp line-up. The reason for this is that, as Thomson alluded to in *Melody Maker* in January 1975, Hodgson and Davies were the driving force of Supertramp because they were the songwriters. Of course, all five members of Supertramp made the band as awesome as it was but equally, when it came to executive decisions and doing interviews, Davies and Hodgson seem to have been more prominent. It is for this reason that I have included Roger Hodgson's brief January 1975 biography at later points in this book because he was quoted in a way that offers a lot of insight into the inner workings of the band and their albums up to that point.

In January 1975, *Melody Maker* provided a list of instruments and equipment that everyone in the band was using at the time. Admittedly, a lot of the content of this list is beyond my understanding but it feels necessary to include this information because I trust that some people will consider it to be of interest. It may not be a definitive list as in, it could have changed upon the release of later albums (that is to say that this list was compiled after the release of *Crime Of The Century*, Hodgson was no longer playing bass for the band by then and in later albums, the use of instruments may have changed according to preferences ranging from technology available, personnel or simply creativity).

Okay, so here's the list, as was presented in

Melody Maker at the time; Rick Davies; Wurlitzer Electric Piano, Hammond M162 organ, two Leslie 760 cabinets, Acoustic 470 amplifier, two custom 2 by 12 JBL cabinets, Helpinstall piano pick up. Roger Hodgson; Fender Stratocaster, Fender electric 12 string, Fender acoustic 12 string, Yamaha acoustic guitar, Fender Dual Showman amplifier, two custom 2 by 12 JBL cabinets, Maestro Echoplex, De Armand wah/volume pedal, Tibetan bells. John Helliwell; Elka Rhapsody string synthesiser, Conn baritone sax, Selmer Mk 6 tenor sax, Le Blanc alto sax, Rene Gounod soprano sax, Selmer clarinet, Yamaha flute, Maestro Octivider, De Armand pedal. Dougie Thomson; Fender jazz bass, Rickenbacker Stereo bass, Fender Dual Showman amplifier, Fender 400 Reflex cabinet, Fender fuzz pedal, Crybaby wah-wah. Bob Benberg; Ludwig bass drum, Gretsch snare, Ludwig toms, two Premier timbales, Paiste and Avedis Zildjian cymbals, wood blocks, Selmer custom sticks.

Okay, back in the room readers! A long, detailed, complex list but I believe that it has value in how it exemplifies how multitalented the band was as an ensemble.

The musical versatility of Supertramp, both in terms of the band's talent pool of multiple instrumentalists and in terms of musical output, was such that to describe the music of Supertramp isn't easy. There is so much to what they created that it takes quite a bit of skill to explain it so well. It could even be argued that their music defies words. In such regard, the following concert review from *Billboard* in May 1977 is an excellent description of what Supertramp sounds like. For anyone who had never heard their music before, I would suggest that the reporter who was lucky enough to see the concert in question pretty much hit the nail on the head when describing Supertramp's music; "A five man band that sound like a million. Supertramp brought its uniquely multi-layered sound here 28th April, providing a blockbuster ninety minute, fourteen song set to an enthusiastic crowd. The group's music is one of complexity and texture — many musical elements woven around a rock base with a sophistication that gives it a classical feel. Each song is built around a fairly simply melody, expanding outward movements through the use of lush vocal harmonies, various wind instruments played by John Helliwell and multiple keyboards (Rick Davies, Roger Hodgson and occasionally Helliwell). Hodgson also served as lead guitarist and Davies moved constantly from acoustic to electric keyboards, leaving bassist Dougie Thomson and Bob C. Benberg on drums as the constants. The possibility of bogging down in a monotony of pretty mush was avoided by the variety of musical bases each excursion used and an abundance of lyrical and melodic hooks. From the classic be-bop of 'Ain't Nobody But Me' or 'Give A Little Bit' (shades of Buddy Holly) to the bluesy feel of 'From Now On' or the satanic 'Asylum', there is seemingly no end to the variety of styles and moods its music explores. The use of two vocalists also provided an interesting contrast. Hodgson's voice has a slightly straining plaintive quality most effective on tunes such as 'Sister Moonshine' where the emotional feel was accentuated by Helliwell's waily (sic) clarinet. Davies offers a tougher, more grounded style with a touch of dryness that added shades of humour to songs such as 'Bloody Well Right' and an emotional balance to Hodgson's more romantic style. The excitement of the finale 'Fool's Overture' was heightened by a film collage which used an in and out of focus giant television screen effect to jump through thematic flashes. Returning after a resounding ovation, the band offered a characteristic contrast with the quietly romantic 'Two Of Us' and the cosmic 'Crime Of The Century' with its stunning visual logo filling the screen behind them."

Notably, with the article having been written in 1977, Supertramp were just getting started on what was to become an arguably groundbreaking discography. However, it is still the case that the concert review pretty much surmises what Supertramp and their music are about overall; talented musicians being creative across a range of genres with plenty of added on-stage visuals.

An early promotional photo from 1971.
From left: Roger Hodgson, Richard Palmer-James, Robert Millar,
Dave Winthrop & Rick Davies.

Chapter Two:
Supertramp (1970)

Supertramp (1970)

Richard Davies – keyboards, harmonica, backing and lead vocals
Roger Hodgson – bass guitar, acoustic guitar, cello, flageolet, lead and backing vocals
Richard Palmer – electric guitar, acoustic guitar, balalaika, backing and lead vocals
Robert Millar – drums

Side one
1. Surely
2. It's A Long Road
3. Aubade/And I Am Not Like Other Birds Of Prey
4. Words Unspoken
5. Maybe I'm A Beggar
6. Home Again

Side two
7. Nothing To Show
8. Shadow Song
9. Try Again
10. Surely (reprise)

The story of how Supertramp became even a possibility really begins with Dutch millionaire, Stanley "Sam" August Miesegaes. Up until 1969 he had been providing financial support to another band, The Joint. However, The Joint weren't living up to his expectations and in wanting to invest in a different project, the millionaire offered band member Rick Davies, a Swindon born keyboard player, the funding to start a new band. It was on the condition that Davies called it a day with The Joint and began a new band completely afresh.

Music had always been a tremendous part of Davies' formative years. Richard Davies was born to Betty and Dick Davies in Wiltshire in 1944. Dick was a merchant navy man and Betty was a hairdresser who considered that with the exception of music, Richard (Rick) wasn't very good at other subjects at school. Rick's interest in music began when he was eight years old; his parents gave him a second hand radiogram as a present and there were a few records that came with it. They included *Drummin' Man* by Gene Krupa. This was a considerable influence on Rick, so much so that by the age of twelve he had joined the British Railways Staff Association Brass and Silver Jubilee Band as a snare drummer. He had heard the drums marching along the street in his hometown and he was hooked. He wanted to take music seriously and with that came drum lessons. However, it was the keyboard that really grabbed Rick's attention and after having a go with that, he excelled on it, even though he didn't take lessons in that instrument.

Rick was quoted in April 1975 in *Beat Instrumental*; "I joined the local brass band in Swindon for experience and it was alright until they wanted me to wear a uniform. Then I packed it in — and that was when I became aware of image I suppose. My mother was always working in her hairdressing shop so I used to go to my auntie's for tea and she had a piano so I started tinkling about on it and learned to play, mainly boogie woogie 'cause that was easiest to pick up, and that way I built it up."

Having dabbled in a range of musical styles, by 1959 Rick was leaning much more towards rock 'n' roll. He joined a band called Vince And The Vigilantes that featured Ginger Frantic on vocals. It was in 1962, whilst he was studying art at Swindon College, that he formed his own band called Rick's Blues. He was by this point a keyboard player and not a drummer. Although Davies was at art school at the time, his focus on music was to the extent that he placed an order for a Hohner electric piano with the aim of Rick's Blues being a rhythm and blues based band but frustratingly for him, most of the rest of the band didn't want to take the step towards playing music professionally. That said, Gilbert O'Sullivan, who was also at the college with Rick, played drums for the band (he was later the best man at Davies' wedding).

In a television interview with Des O'Connor in March 1972, O'Sullivan asserted that it was Davies who taught him to play both drums and piano. Rick disbanded Rick's Blues when his father became ill. His priorities had changed because he needed to leave college in order to get a job. He worked as a welder at a company called Square D; they made industrial control products and systems. Rick's father passed away in 1973. Hopes of a career in music were probably considerably compromised for Rick at that time. That said, factory life was probably not for him. He was quoted in *Melody Maker* in June 1979; "I think I was scared off by the Beatles. What changed that? Fear. Fear of being slung back into the factory."

Also, Rick was quoted in August 1977 in *New Musical Express*; "When you start out it's an adventure. You're young kids and it's a chance to get out and almost be swashbuckling about it. It's one of the few remaining outlets for that kind of thing, because everything else these days is so regulated and worked out. Generally, people can't go out and discover a new land or be as romantic as they could in the old days, but as a young band, you can. I think you just grow up a bit. You're still in a young world, even though you're not young. It's the dilemma of the ageing rock star. It's hard to shake off the fact that somebody could break his leg, or walk out, and I'm too old to start again. It would scare the hell out of me. It's fear and insecurity. I can remember the jolt of going into a factory after spending five years at art school. It nearly put me in the madhouse. Now I'm afraid of not making it, in a way. I hate those stories about great big stars now working in gas stations. They just sicken me. So and so's blown all his money on coke, I just think, that's ridiculous."

Davies had an extent of determination that would ultimately serve him well, from the beginning of his career and beyond. In 1966 he became the organist for a band called The Lonely Ones (one of Noel Redding's earliest bands. Redding had left though by the time Davies joined). The band's drummer, Keith Bailey invited Rick to join. Rick was quoted in *Beat Instrumental* in April 1975; "That was Noel Redding's band. He had just left as I came in, which I suppose is quite nice for me now. I don't think I could have taken that then. The whole band was a bit like Noel, it was full of young kids out for a good time."

Rick's time with The Lonely Ones turned out to be less than fruitful. In the same article he was quoted as he described the band's activity on the Continent as "disintegrated" as he explained, "I went back to Geneva to try and salvage the band because a couple of the guys thought it was worth saving, but it was hopeless and I decided to form a band round myself."

It was this experience of Rick's that got the ball rolling in terms of being a band leader and hence his founding of ultimately, Supertramp. Rick's time with other bands was not wasted though, at least not musically. It was during this time that he was writing material that would find a place with Supertramp. He was quoted in the same *Beat Instrumental* feature; "I started writing a few instrumentals when I was with the semi-pro band. I was influenced by good R and B — Chuck Berry, Fats Domino, Bill Doggett — then I just stopped completely. Things did change though when I started doing that film music, it was a little broader than R and B, it had to be, so I started thinking about different chords and I suppose there was a bit of classical music in it."

Ironically perhaps, as Davies' musical repertoire increased, seemingly, so did his self criticism; "It's harder to write as you get on because the more you know the harder it is to play something without thinking 'ah no, I've done it before' or 'that's tasteless' because your tastes improve and you become more self critical. I often write things and just scrap them, that's happened a lot. I just write when I can."

Davies later admitted that he had to blag his way into The Lonely Ones a bit; he lied about his organ playing abilities in order to get into the band. I guess he learnt on the job because the recordings of Davies playing the organ in Supertramp certainly don't seem to convey any difficulties! The Lonely Ones later changed their name to The Joint.

Things were taking off; the band was involved with sessions for the soundtracks to be used in German movies. Rick Davies was quoted in *Sounds* in December 1975; "We worked in England for about six months playing soul stuff, then we went to Europe for supposedly two weeks but we got stuck there, (we) didn't come back for a year and a half! We were gigging at night and making film music during the day. It was good experience but Germans make the worst films in the world. We were just a cheap way for them to get music on their films. We worked for a guy called David Lluellyn, who was an unbelievable character we met over there. He used to get us all these film jobs. The band were broke when Dave mentioned the fact that he knew this guy in Switzerland who was a millionaire. We thought 'sure pull the other one', but then again it was worth a try. We were all destitute at the PN Club living on soup. We'd play at the weekends and that would give us enough money to last us through 'till Thursday then we had to pilfer until Saturday. It was on a Saturday that Dave went to see this guy and then he just didn't get in contact for about three months and we thought 'that's it, he's gone', then we got a telephone call from Dave saying that the guy would be interested in seeing us. We couldn't believe it! We were all walking around in a dream thinking 'this is it'."

Davies was quoted in *Sounds* in December 1975: "He had these ideas for us to get classical themes and turn them into pop music. Of course we all went charging down to his house and when we got there we spent the first two weeks playing ping-pong. We had an attempt at getting this thing together. It was completely bizarre, this guy's music and the pop idea on top of it. We eventually came over and signed to Robert Stigwood and ended up playing the Rasputin Club every week, that was about it."

Things were about to take a constructive turn though. Davies was quoted in the same feature; "One morning Sam phoned me up at nine o' clock in the morning and told me to have a look out of the window and I said, 'there's nothing out there, except an old coach' and he said, 'it's yours boys', so we got in and Andy (our singer) drove it around Finchley while we played football in the back. It's only when we started playing the Marquee that it got to be a problem. We had to park in Oxford Street and you'd see a huge chain of people on Wardour Street carrying equipment, anyway that was taken away from us when something wasn't pleasing Sam. I went over to see what was grieving him."

It turned out that Sam had high expectations and the group were not living up to them. Davies was quoted in the same interview in *Sounds*; "I knew the band wasn't that good, but everyone was heartbroken when we had to split, we were so close." The band just wasn't to the satisfaction of Stanley August Miesegaes. He wanted a greater return on his investment and as a result, he offered to invest just in Rick Davies and not the rest of the group. It was on the absolute condition that Davies left The Joint and agreed to start a new band. Luckily for Davies, Sam believed in him and was happy to back him, just not the rest of the band.

Davies continued, "I went over to Sam's to try and write my own music, so I could get enough confidence to start something off my own back and I stayed there just writing. Of course all sorts of crazy ideas popped up from Sam, like "Rick Around The World In Eighty Tunes" whereby we'd hire a few Land Rovers and go round the world. We'd sit in an Afghanistan village and be influenced by the music and then go onto somewhere else. It sounded fantastic but it wasn't real at all. So I went back to London and I began auditioning (other musicians) for what was to become the first Supertramp." As far as millionaires go, Sam sounds very eccentric. Well meaning and helpful perhaps, but certainly eccentric.

That's where the rest of the band that would come to be known as Supertramp come into the story. Rick Davies placed an advert in *Melody Maker* in the search for musicians to join his band. Rick was quoted in *New Musical Express* in February 1975; "I knew what I wanted in the way of musicians, personality-wise, and what I wanted them to play. Also at that time, when I finally got back, there were a lot of things happening musically — like Jethro Tull, King Crimson and Traffic. I was really into that, because before I was only listening to Americans really."

Enter the team of Roger Hodgson on bass and vocals, Richard Palmer on guitars and vocals and Keith Baker on drums. During the brief time that the band was called Daddy, Keith Baker was replaced by Robert Miller, a former stage actor. Of all of the new members that would eventually be going by the name of Supertramp, it was Roger Hodgson who Rick Davies clicked with musically. Despite their different backgrounds, there was definitely some serious chemistry there and it was this that would ultimately lead to a musical partnership that would see Supertramp go on to have tremendous success. Whilst Davies was from a working class background and his musical interests were in blues and jazz, Hodgson had gone straight into the music business after leaving public school and was more into pop music.

Roger Hodgson, ex-pupil of Buckingham's Stowe School, began his musical career at the age of thirteen as he progressed through school bands. He was quoted in January 1975 in *Melody Maker*; "It started when my parents got divorced and my mum managed to steal my dad's guitar from him without him seeing. I think if that hadn't happened I wouldn't have taken up guitar." Some elements of Hodgson's musical training were based on having had piano lessons but predominantly, it seems that he achieved a lot from a self-taught perspective.

As he was quoted in *Piano News* in January 2011, "We had a genuine grand piano at home. But my parents didn't want me to play on it. I can't even tell you why. I took piano lessons from age sixteen and had to learn pieces from the classical repertoire at first. But, to be honest, I didn't always find that very interesting. I much rather wanted to play my own compositions and developed my own style which of course was very different from that classical-romantic style. I do have a very distinct musical power of imagination, I hear the music in my head, I'm hearing the chords and melodies and I immediately know where to find them on the piano."

Hodgson was quoted in *Record Mirror* in August 1970; "As far as my personal history is concerned I've had a passion for playing guitar since my early schooldays — and it certainly affected my work! At school they tried to dissuade my passion for music, but in the end they let me have my own solo concert. I was twelve at the time. I played most of my own compositions but the only encore I received was the one non-original song I performed — Cliff Richard's 'Bachelor Boy'. I left school at eighteen and joined a group called People Like Us, but I was always the odd one out because I refused to force a smile on stage. Lionel Conway of Island Records heard a demo we made and asked me to leave the group and make a solo record of one of my own compositions called 'Mr Boyd'. It was released in America under the name Argosy and got to number twenty-eight in the Kansas City charts." That record is pretty rare now! You would easily need to have a good few hundred pounds spare to commit to making any kind of realistic bid on it.

Roger was quoted in May 2006 in the *Times Herald* as he described what his first meeting with Rick Davies was like; "His manager put a big advertisement in a very famous English music paper (*Melody Maker*). I answered it along with a few hundred other musicians. When I arrived, Rick was sitting in a corner, kind of exhausted. He told me he was really impressed by my voice. We had a chance afterwards to go for a drink, and the seeds of Supertramp were sewn that day."

Hodgson was quoted in *Sounds* in December 1975 as he recalled the day he teamed up with Rick Davies. That very same day, Hodgson had already signed a contract with DJM to record the single under the band name of Argosy; "When I joined Rick I had signed a contract with another guy the very same day. The single had Elton John on piano, Nigel Olsson on drums and Caleb Quaye on guitar… it also flopped… Tony Blackburn liked it."

When Hodgson first worked with Davies, his main instrument was actually bass guitar, in the same interview he was quoted; "That's my favourite instrument funnily enough, I love the bass more than any other instrument" (It's plausible that this may not be the case now, over a long and innovative career, Hodgson played a lot of instruments. In *Piano News* in January 2011, he was quoted as he advocated passionately on what other instruments meant to him; "There are pianos that sing very wonderfully and where you think 'Ah, how beautiful!' Then I become at one with the instrument and let the sounds take me. But then again, there are instruments which leave me completely cold. Sound and character of an instrument definitely do have a great impact on composing. The keyboard naturally allows very different tone colours and effects from the piano and my keyboard pieces mostly have a quicker rhythmic pulse. Think about 'Dreamer' where the chords get repeated in fast tempo.").

From the point of having auditioned Hodgson, Davies had begun writing with him. Richard Palmer (who ultimately became most famous for his work with King Crimson) was the third writer, he composed the lyrics for the band's first and eponymously titled album. Palmer actually recalled in later interviews that nobody really wanted to write the lyrics for the album but he did so reluctantly because he pretty much drew the short straw for that side of the creative process.

Roger Hodgson was quoted on the matter in *Classic Rock Revisited* in February 2012; "I didn't have confidence that I could write lyrics. I read some of the lyrics now that I did write, and I put out on those early Supertramp albums, and I cringe. As I got to know myself more I got comfortable. I had to learn how to get inside and express myself. I started out trying to write about things that were not true to myself and it didn't work. It was not something that came naturally but it slowly evolved."

Endearingly, overall, the differences between Rick and Roger were ultimately key ingredients in what would become the musical and writing chemistry between them. As Hodgson was quoted in November 2007 in *Goldmine*, "It was very much that the magic or the essence of Supertramp was the kind of yin-yang polarity of Rick's songwriting and my songwriting and our two musical styles. I mean, Rick was five years older than me, so he had grown up on the music of jazz and blues. That was his background, and that's where he gravitated towards, where I grew up on The Beatles and more the pop rock. But actually, when we played together, there was an incredible empathy between the two of us, when it was just the two of us, and it was very magical, especially earlier on when there weren't too many other people around and it was, literally, just the two of us. And I think as we developed as songwriters, we started writing, obviously, totally separately, but I think just having that competition, healthy competition, we wanted to give the best of ourselves, and having another writer in the band kind of gave that sense of competition that really did bring out the best in us."

Daddy changed their name to Supertramp whilst doing concerts in Germany in order to avoid being confused with another band on the circuit at the time who went by the name of Daddy Longlegs. The Supertramp moniker came from a book by William Henry Davies called, *The Autobiography Of A Supertramp.*

As comfortable as Supertramp were with performing live, the rehearsal process for their first album at a country house in Kent was perhaps a little more stilted in terms of how nobody seemed keen to write the lyrics for the band's original material (bearing in mind that the band's live set at the time consisted of covers as well as original material). The eponymous Supertramp album was recorded only during particular hours of the day; it had to be done between 12am and 6am because of a superstition they held that those were the best hours in which to have the magic for making music. Well, that and the fact that at the time it was rumoured that Traffic and Spooky Tooth recorded their music at such hours and seemingly it worked for them. It probably wasn't plain sailing though; not everyone involved in the process was nocturnal and it wasn't unusual for the sound engineer, Robin Black, to struggle to stay awake at such hours.

Roger Hodgson was quoted in August 1970 in *Record Mirror* as he discussed what the band's tour schedule was like at the time; "We're very pleased at the reaction we've had to our initial bookings in Britain at places like the Marquee. As a group we haven't been in existence for long, although all of the members have had a good deal of musical schooling in various groups during the past few years. When we originally got together earlier this year it was decided that we must spend some months together tightening up our sound before doing British gigs, so we went to the Continent and spent several weeks rehearsing solidly in Geneva. Then we spent some time as a resident band at the PN club in Munich. We had five half-hour shows during the week and seven shows a day at weekends. This was very good for us; it's the type of experience that many other bands have gone through at the beginning of their careers. For some reason, a lot of really good British outfits consider that the hard, exhausting work in German clubs is one of the best methods of tightening group sound and getting the group together as a team. We certainly found that to be true. Now we're looking forward to all our British gigs and are really keen to hear the reaction to our album when it's released. All the numbers were written by ourselves."

Rick Davies was quoted in *Sounds* in December 1975 as he offered some context on what was going on in the musical scene during the early days of Supertramp; "There was a huge change happening at the time I was away in Europe. That change was like Traffic, Jethro Tull, Spooky Tooth, sort of nice up and coming bands, which I wasn't aware of until I went down to see Rory Gallagher and Taste at the Lyceum, only then did I reckon on the possibilities that something could happen, because I didn't rate myself as a big pop star and I thought to get anywhere I was going to have to be like that. But with the new bands coming up, there was a new standard to live up to and that's what we were aiming for. Roger, Richard and Bob were all aware of these groups, so having them in the band was sort of an education for me. It was great because Richard Palmer was going on about Traffic and The Band, getting into their lyrics and I had never thought about their lyrics before."

It is plausible that Supertramp didn't hold the songs from their first album in particularly high regard. When *Crime Of The Century* became a big part of the band's live set, all of the songs from the first album were dropped from the live set. Very occasionally 'Home Again' and 'Surely' were referred to in encores briefly but that was as far as the band went with paying homage to their earlier material once the *Crime Of The Century* album had got the ball rolling for them commercially in 1974.

Songs from Supertramp's first album are still certainly worthy of attention though, not only is the album worth a listen in its own right but also, the songs 'Words Unspoken' and 'I Am Not Like Other Birds Of Prey' were featured as part of the soundtrack for the 1971 British film, *Extremes*. Also, as much as Supertramp were yet to take off commercially, their first album received a positive response on the basis of the music itself. They were one of the first bands to be signed to the UK branch of A&M Records. Whilst their first album was released with the label on 14th July 1970, it would not see an American release until late 1977.

During the whole period surrounding the band's first album, personnel changes were frequent. David Winthrop, on flute and saxophone, joined the group shortly after the release of their first album and not long after Supertramp had performed at the Isle of Wight Festival in 1970. For the following six months, the band's membership was under continual change. This included Palmer leaving the band as well as Millar, who suffered a nervous breakdown after Supertramp's tour of Norway. Kevin Currie, a Liverpool drummer who was with Supertramp for only a relatively brief period, was quoted in *Sounds* in August 1971 as he described the problems with the personnel in the band over the period of their first album; "Yeah, it just wasn't happening personally for the group at that time. It got so bad that the drummer had a nervous breakdown and at the time of recording the first album. Everybody hated each other's guts. Considering all that it came out pretty well. It was a very melancholy kind of thing and the mood of the group fitted the music. That's why people dug it I think."

In the liner notes of their second album, Supertramp described their first album as having had a "melancholy mood". Their first album seemed to lack any particular direction in terms of theme and concept. It feels more like an exploratory statement. As Davies was quoted in *Sounds* in December 1975; "We were very green then. There was this thing about not having a producer. Bands weren't using producers then, and we decided 'yeah we're not going to have a producer, Paul McCartney's not using a producer, why should we use one?' it was that sort of greenness."

By greenness, in the context of what was being said, I'm going to assume that Davies was getting at the idea that the album felt musically organic rather than particularly focused thematically. In the same article, Hodgson advocated that for the band's first album, the organic and somewhat unfocused approach wasn't a problem; "It worked on the first one, it had its own kind of magic."

The individuality between Hodgson and Davies was seemingly apparent from early on. Hodgson was quoted as he described the band's living situation whilst recording their first album; "In that first year we were put in a country house together, we didn't mix socially and the vibes got really bad. We never made any friends because the vibes were so bad, people hated coming up to the house."

The early days of the band were such that they had yet to really establish a mutually agreed sense of direction. As Roger Hodgson was quoted in *Goldmine* in November 2007, "We were still trying to find out who we were, and there were three of us writing the songs, Rick and I had just met, so we were just trying to find a way to write together and so it was... yeah, we were just trying to find our feet."

Regarding the period of working on their first album together, Davies was quoted in *Sounds* in December 1975; "That first year, we must have played to an awful lot of people. We were doing *Top Gear* all the time, it was keeping us alive." In the same article, Hodgson was quoted; "Our first album did sell quite a lot", to which Davies clarified, "Yeah it did. It almost took off in actual fact, because we did the Croydon Greyhound where we pulled in a lot of people just once, after that Bob left and then it just crashed." Close but not quite close enough. Still though, a good start that would ultimately get the ball rolling for the band.

PINK FAIRIES
PLUS
SUPERTRAMP
AND
SIDEWINDER
MALVERN WINTER GARDENS
OCTOBER 30TH
TICKETS 60p - AT DOOR 70p
Available from :
The Winter Gardens Box Office and
The Music Centre, Worcester.
A Cherry Red Presentation

Chapter Three:
Indelibly Stamped (1971)

Supertramp's second album was so different to their first. Davies was quoted in *Sounds* in December 1975; "The second album consisted of a different band. By that time Richard Palmer and Bob Millar had left. We got a guy called Dave Winthrop on saxophone, Kevin Currie on drums and Frank Farrel on bass."

Such change of line-up may have been a factor in how the second album was stylistically different to the first. However, with the first album not really having taken off in the way that Hodgson and Davies had perhaps hoped for, it may have been the case that the writing duo decided between themselves to do something different for the second album. Short term drummer, Kevin

Currie, was quoted in *Sounds* in August 1971 as he discussed the musical direction (or perhaps lack thereof) present on the band's second album. It comes across that there was perhaps a lot of experimentation and uncertainty in terms of having any sense of particular artistic focus; "We all really dug Free and Paul (Kossoff) came down to the country and had a blow and he played a gig with us but that was it… We're still basically a rock band and we don't want to change that but there isn't any one set direction because we have so many ideas and influences which we'll have to get together. Everyone is more concerned with melody and this album we're working on now shows exactly where we're at."

In an interview with *Record Mirror* in May 1971, Roger Hodgson was quoted in a promotional interview that he did prior to the release of *Indelibly Stamped*; "We'll be rehearsing now for a few weeks, then we got to the PN Club, Munich for a few weeks to break the band in to coincide with the release of the album. What can I say about the album… it's right where we all are at the moment. We're not out to impress all and sundry with our musical prowess, virtuosity, etc. We like to think people who buy the album will listen with their heads, not their ears, but we don't mind. If they get something out of it what we didn't consciously put on it, then good for them. We think it is quite a varied album, both on the album and on stage. The fact that Supertramp are still together is a minor miracle in itself. When the first album was being made the personnel scenes were really bad. Vans and cars breaking down one after the other… We had a gas doing the album. We were in the studios all over Easter and we wrote and produced it ourselves. People don't realise it but the studios and studio engineers all affect the way the album comes together. It was recorded at Olympic in Barnes, which is a really nice studio, and the engineer Bob knew exactly what we were trying to do without anyone having to say anything. A&M are rush releasing it to get it out for early June. So we can only sit tight and hope everyone digs it."

The days when people were allowed to admit that a rush release was due to happen rather than adding it only as a footnote after release when something is poorly received! Nevertheless, an interesting interview where Hodgson made it clear (as he would do so many times in interviews throughout his career) that the music came first, the thought for the commercial direction of it came second.

The second album signified a considerable change towards a more simplistic style of rock music. By the band's own admission in the liner notes, the song 'Travelled' is the only one on the album that bears any resemblance to the material on their previous album (Hodgson was quoted in *Jam* in September 1983; "When Supertramp started out, we never had a conscious goal apart from just trying to do everything the best way that we could.").

Again though, this album, like their first, wasn't a commercial success. It was over a decade later, once Supertramp had acquired commercial success through their later work, that *Indelibly Stamped* was certified gold in France and Canada. Original LP releases of *Indelibly Stamped* aren't that common, the distinctive feature being that of a coloured gatefold cover and the band's name being in a different font to the title of the album. The album cover features the torso of a tattooed topless woman. The image can be enjoyed in all its uncensored glory on the UK release of the album but in the US, A&M opted to paste two gold stars over the nipples.

Hodgson apparently considered that at the time, the purpose of *Indelibly Stamped* was for the band to get back in the good books of their management after their first album. As a result, the making of *Indelibly Stamped* was perhaps somewhat haphazard, with new members, Kevin Currie, Frank Farrell, and Dave Winthrop being recruited to the band at the last minute, not long before the actual recording sessions for the album began. Once again, as with the first album, Supertramp did a tour for *Indelibly Stamped* in Germany at the PN Club in Munich. As with many British bands who were trying to make it in Germany due to the perceived lack of opportunity in the British music scene at the time, the performances were often received with variable levels of appreciation from rowdy audiences who weren't always in attendance for the music itself. At this stage in their career, Supertramp were very much still in the formative years of their journey to success.

Live gigs during the period of Supertramp's second album were certainly humble and not full of the audience appreciation that the band would ultimately go on to receive. Davies was quoted in *Sounds* in December 1975; "It was all rock 'n' roll really. We used to get people up on the bloody stage and it was just chaos, bopping away doing about three encores, but there was meat and potatoes behind it. No more or less people would come to the next gig."

In August 1971 in *Sounds*, the reporter, Ray Telford, philosophised on his curiosity that Supertramp were still going after their first album; "As their publicity handout truthfully observes, it is a minor miracle that Supertramp are still together. Indeed they have a good name and I feel it is this alone which has kept them together more than anything. Their first album gained them a hard core of followers especially on the college circuit but Kevin (Currie) reasons that that type of audience is a limitation on the group."

In such regard, Currie was quoted; "Most of our live gigs have been college dates which means we're only exposed to people who want to know about us anyway. Recently though, we've played some northern gigs at things like Mecca Ballrooms and really straight sort of clubs and the receptions have been great. These are the kind of people that wouldn't normally associate themselves with groovy college bands. We've still got a good name and even the people who haven't seen us come along and they expect something good. Yeah, I think they're getting it too."

It comes across that Kevin Currie was quite the diplomat and even though he wasn't in Supertramp for very long, he was quite possibly a key instigator of keeping the peace and harmony in the band from a personnel perspective. Rick Davies was quoted as he spoke of Currie in *New Musical Express* in February 1975; "Unless he'd come in, we'd probably have folded again. We needed someone to believe in what the band was doing. He really got us believing in ourselves again. He sort of served a purpose and went. I think he was a bit sick about it really. When he left, we talked about disbanding. It was only then that we realised it was our music and our songs and nobody else was going to do it. So…"

In the same feature, Roger Hodgson was quoted as being keen to credit other people for being strong instigators in keeping Supertramp from completely disbanding; "The fact the band kept going was nothing to do with us. You have to have the business side to get the music through, and if it had been down to us it would never have happened. When we talked about splitting and the drummer and sax player left, it was really Doug the bass player and our sound mixer guy who got their heads together and said, 'Right. It's time we started sorting things out'."

Indelibly Stamped was released in June 1971 in both the UK and the US. Unfortunately though, it sold less than their previous album and as a result, Miesegaes decided to stop funding them in October 1972. As a result, all members of the band went their separate ways, all members that is except Rick Davies and Roger Hodgson. Perhaps they had more belief in where they could take Supertramp in the long run or maybe a career in the music industry was all they'd ever known and/or wanted (particularly with Roger having been in the industry since leaving school and with Rick not wanting to go back to working in a factory). Whatever the reasons, it's a good thing that Rick and Roger had decided not to give up on Supertramp. There was certainly more to come.

Even though A & M in America released this promotional single from *Indelibly Stamped* they were clearly still familiarising themselves with their British signing as they credited it as being from the first album.

Chapter Four:
Crime Of The Century (1974)

**Crime Of The Century
(1974)**

Rick Davies – keyboards,
harmonica, lead and
backing vocals
Roger Hodgson – electric
and acoustic guitars,
keyboards, lead and
backing vocals
John Helliwell –
saxophones, clarinet,
backing vocals, glass harp
and celesta
Dougie Thomson – bass
guitar
Bob C. Benberg – drums

Side one
1. School
2. Bloody Well Right
3. Hide In Your Shell
4. Asylum

Side two
5. Dreamer
6. Rudy
7. If Everyone Was Listening
8. Crime Of The Century

After two albums that had been a commercial failure and funding having been withdrawn by their sponsor, Hodgson and Davies were in a dilemma as to how to proceed. Continuing with Supertramp would have been harder than before without the financial backing and the need to form a new band was such that a lengthy audition process was inevitable in order to get things just right.

However, on the good side of things, Supertramp were still supported by A&M Records and as a result, if the band wanted to continue then the opportunity was still there for Hodgson and Davies in some form. Hodgson was quoted in *Classic Rock Revisited* in February 2012; "We were very,

very fortunate to have a record label that believed in supporting the artist and letting the artist develop. A&M Records, especially Jerry Moss, he really believed in us. He probably lost money the first few albums, but he allowed us to take as much time as we needed in the studio because he believed in us and he saw the potential. It was much more common in those days than it is these days, obviously."

Dave Margereson certainly still had faith in the band. He already worked for A&M and began working more closely with Supertramp as their manager. He would continue in the role for the next ten years. Such was his confidence in the band that he sent the new line-up to a seventeenth century farm in Dorset to rehearse together and prepare for a new album.

John Helliwell was quoted in *Sounds* in December 1975 as he recalled how they acquired access to the premises from which to work on *Crime Of The Century*; "After the rehearsal studios in the Old Kent Road, we used to rehearse under Kew Bridge. Then we got together with A&M Records who hired a cottage for us in Somerset, we managed to wangle a stay there. So we all went there with girlfriends, wives, kids and cats. We were there for about three months trying to get a producer together."

As Hodgson was quoted in *Goldmine* in November 2007, "It was the fashion of that time. Traffic had done it, and so we wanted to do it. We wanted to be put in a farmhouse and just live together for a few months to really bond and come up with something really great, and that's what we did." Ultimately, the album that came to be titled *Crime Of The Century* was recorded at several studios including Ramport Studios (owned by The Who) and Trident Studios.

It is fascinating to consider that whilst *Crime Of The Century* consisted of eight tracks, Davies and Hodgson had actually recorded over forty demo songs (some of which appeared on the band's later albums, *Crisis? What Crisis?* and *…Famous Last Words…*). The very fact that so many demos were recorded during the making of *Crime Of The Century* is, I believe, suggestive of potentially two things, 1) the tremendous talents of Davies and Hodgson and 2) the idea that they were probably very determined to make a good go of things after their first two albums hadn't quite hit the nail on the head.

Roger Hodgson was quoted in February 1975 in *New Musical Express* as he explained what Sam's funding had meant for the band during the days that it was there; "The first two years were a complete dream… it does make the whole band's history very unique. When we started we had everything. All the equipment we wanted. We travelled about in a forty two-seater coach with beds in the back. We didn't have the physical discomforts that most bands do when they start off. Then when Sam left, we did experience physical discomfort. Like the money went down to nothing, and the equipment broke up."

In the same article, Rick Davies was quoted on the matter; "We'd always had someone to lean on with money and it took us a long time to accept that we had to make our own way." When the interviewer asked Davies if they relied on Sam too much, he replied that they did; "Yeah, there's no way you can't when you have somebody like that. It's like when you have a big record... well, this (*Crime Of The Century*) is the first experience we've had of any big sales, but already signs of leaning on that are creeping in. It's something you've got to be careful of. A lot of musicians are really lazy and, speaking personally, you tend to grab any security that's going because you know what the business is like."

Hodgson was quoted as he added, "You can get very complacent if you know a wage is coming in. And the vibe in the band at that time wasn't really a group feeling..." It's fascinating to think that perhaps Sam's removal of funding may have given the band some drive to up their game in terms of thinking about what was needed commercially to give them the best chance of success. That said, musically, the confidence may have always been there. As Davies was quoted in the same article, "I think there was always an underlying confidence in the material we'd done. We didn't just freak out and say, 'Oh we can't go on', we just went on... You play music you enjoy and hope people are going to enjoy that."

When Sam made the decision to stop funding Supertramp, for Rick Davies in particular, it had a significant influence on his artistic process as a musician. Where time and resources had previously been there in abundance, it was now a case of needing to get things working well. It was sink or swim basically. As Davies was quoted in *Sounds* in December 1975; "There was almost too much wasted time, you get to rely on that big money man, there's no urgency, your life doesn't depend on it. By the time we left him I thought 'wow we could sink like a stone'!"

Rick was quoted as he described his living conditions during the period after Sam's funding had stopped; "That was really bizarre when we had that house, the big house in Holland Villas. This big house, Joe Cocker was in there and there was only supposed to be four people to pay the rent, which was astronomical, so there was twelve of us in the end. There were people in the roof all over the place. I was living in the shower. You should have seen the scene when the landlady came around to collect the rent. I've never seen anything like it. She came around about ten in the morning, and it was like panicsville. The alarm went off, I got up, walked straight out of the door with my pullover on, it was pouring with rain and I just walked round Shepherd's Bush. I didn't have money for breakfast or anything. I ended up bumming a quid off that guy at the Cabin. I expected everyone to be out in the street when I got back. I was surprised, everyone was still there. It was like a farce. People stark naked rushing from room to room as they were showing the landlady around, there were people hiding in the cupboards. They were going to check in the attic and of course there were tents in there!"

After running many auditions to find just the right people, Rick Davies and Roger Hodgson eventually welcomed new band members to the line-up. They were Dougie Thomson on bass (he had already worked with Davies and Hodgson for a year before being officially named as a full member of Supertramp), Bob Siebenberg (credited as Bob C. Benberg) on drums and John Helliwell on woodwind, keyboards and backing vocals. It was with this line-up that Hodgson was able to turn his focus more towards doing keyboard and guitar compositions due to having the bass element of the band covered so capably by Thomson.

This line-up of Supertramp was to remain stable for the next decade. Davies was quoted in *Sounds* in May 1976; "After the second album it was just me and Roger and we got rid of everybody and decided to start over. We took a chance and so far it's been okay. With *Crime Of The Century* it became a whole new thing for us. It took five months to make and was far more heavily produced than anything we had ever done. In fact, people have said they like the first two albums because of their obvious amateurism."

Hodgson was quoted in the Canadian paper, *The Standard* in December 2008; "Actually, that was a very exciting time for us. Just prior to that Rick and I had looked at giving up and going our separate ways, but had decided to give it one more chance… the record company heard demos of some of our songs and heard the potential." In *Goldmine* in November 2007, Hodgson was quoted as he explained which of the demos were perhaps the ones that saved their bacon; "The record company had heard the demos of 'Bloody Well Right' and 'School' and said, 'Hey, there's something here, let's support them'."

Supertramp were featured on the front page of *Melody Maker* in January 1975. Their UK concert dates were listed and it was reported that the tour would continue in America in the spring. It introduced Supertramp as "hot property" and that they were taking "a giant step towards rock 'n' roll stardom" as they were due to hit the road for their first headlining British tour. Peter Bowyer, who was responsible for promoting the tour at the time, was quoted as having said, "I've had my eye on Supertramp for some time. Their concert at London's Victoria Palace in December was a sell-out and I believe they will enter the Yes brackets as one of Britain's major groups. They will break through in a major way in 1975." In the same feature, Dave Margereson was quoted; "I saw them just before the (1973) breakup and, from the two albums they had already made, I knew they had tremendous possibilities."

In *Sounds* in December 1975, Peter Makowski described Dougie Thomson as "a quiet unassuming character. On stage you can see him bouncing around, pumping throbbing bass lines that have become such an essential part of Supertramp's sound." In the same feature, Thomson was quoted; "I joined the Mk II Supertramp about six months before it broke up, immediately before that I was playing in some weird West End strip clubs. I'd played a bit in Alan Bown's band. That was at a weird period of that band's existence, when they parted company with Alan and we tried to get something happening, but we didn't really get anything sorted out at all. So I was just looking around for a job to get some money, and then I saw this ad for Supertramp. Sometime before my brother, who's one of our roadies now, had been to London and brought one of their albums back. So I had been aware of them. I decided to go along and see what was happening. At this point they had been going through some incredible audition scenes. I remember going to the Pied Bull in Islington and there were some terrible scenes. Rick was there with his crash helmet and sleeping bag. Dave Winthrop had given up hope and had gone to play pinball. Roger and Kevin were there trying to get some kind of audition sorted out. So I went in, played my two minutes and left. Roger phoned me up a couple of days later, asking me to come down to his house, and it just kind of evolved from there. It really was a strange period for the band, with Dave Winthrop. Sometimes he just wouldn't come to gigs, and then he'd turn up a couple of gigs later almost as if nothing had happened… very strange."

Bob Siebenberg was quoted in *Sounds* in December 1975 as he recalled how he first met Davies and Hodgson; "We (his previous band) stuck around and watched Supertramp, and they were pretty good. They were the first band that I had seen that I thought were nifty, and I thought I could get on playing with them. After that I was putting it around that they were pretty good. The way I put it was they were the closest thing to Traffic I'd seen, they were really punchy… The next time I saw them was when we were playing a gig in Barnet and I saw their drummer beaming in on me. About two weeks later Roger came up to me in The Kensington and said they were going to be doing a new album in September and the drummer was splitting and what did I think about doing sessions for them."

In the same feature, Siebenberg explained how Supertramp valued rehearsing compared to his last band; "In the Bees (Make Honey) I never rehearsed for one day. We never rehearsed at all. With Supertramp it was different, the complete opposite. I remember the first time we got together was at the Furniture Cave in Kings Road."

Siebenberg was quoted in *Modern Drummer* in December 2014; "The band was brand new. Rick Davies and Roger Hodgson had recorded two albums previously with two different line-ups, without much success. There was a real feeling of optimism in the new line-up, and we jelled right away. We knew we had an interesting cast of characters and totally believed in ourselves. This was the first record with the new line-up and it felt like we could do something special. The ingredients were all there. We had label support and tons of enthusiasm." In the same interview in 2014, he was also quoted; "I would have to admit I've had no rudimental training. It's all seat of the pants. It's how I learned to play — listening, emulating, and feeling. I grew up playing in bands. I never lived anywhere where I could practice."

John Helliwell was quoted in *Sounds* in December 1975 as he recalled how he came to be in Supertramp; "I went home after playing with them and the wife asked me what it was like, and I said 'yeah pretty good but I think I'll go back tomorrow', then I went the next day and came home and she said 'well how do you feel about it now?' I said 'It's alright but I'll have to go again' and it kept on going like that. At the same time I had to do a job during the day. So I enlisted with Manpower and the first job I got was as a petrol pump attendant. Then I got a job screwing nuts and bolts together at a factory in Maidenhead."

In the same feature, when Helliwell was asked to surmise his music career prior to joining Supertramp, he joked to the interviewer, "have you got three more tapes on you?" Such was the extent of his experience even prior to Supertramp. He offered an overview as follows; "I was with Alan Bown for about six years through all the ups and downs, and then after that, when it split up I went and worked for a few strip clubs. No hang on! The first job I got before that was working in a dry cleaning factory during the day and the Celebrity Club at night. Then when I sorted out my tax problem, I left the dry cleaning job and the Celebrity Club and went on to play the Twilight Rooms where Doug was working, and then I got my big break… I joined Jimmy Johnson And The Bandwagon! Then I joined up with Arthur Conley and later on with Jimmy Ruffin. Each one was a step up. Then I went to Germany and I came back in August to join this lot. They said they were making the album in September."

Funnily enough, Helliwell had put his own advert in *Melody Maker* prior to seeing and responding to the one that Rick Davies had put in the same paper (Helliwell was quoted as he relayed the story in *Rock* in September 1983; "It said "Have sax, will travel"). Oh and Helliwell and the Manpower sourced jobs? Well, as Roger Hodgson was quoted in *Rock* in September 1983, "We told John to keep his job at the gas station." That is to say that, as well as being in Supertramp, Hodgson and Davies advised Helliwell not to give up the day job. Not as a comment on his musical ability, far from it! But purely because financially and commercially the band weren't yet stable. They pretty much had no idea if things were going to take off for them to be able to make a living from it.

A lot of time and energy seemed to go on trying to get the band's line-up just right in the early days. The situation was probably less than ideal in allowing them to just get on with making music. Hodgson was quoted in *Jam* in September 1983; "It was very tough to find the right musicians to make Supertramp in the beginning. It took about five years to do and many, many auditions. We must have seen over four hundred drummers, fifty bass players, and about fifty guitarists. For the first five years, I was constantly changing from bass guitar to lead guitar just because we couldn't find whichever one at the time, and whichever one we couldn't find, I would take up that instrument."

It's great how being multitalented and able to play several instruments allowed for Hodgson to be able to accommodate the shortcomings of not having a secure band line-up but still, it can't have been ideal and it must have been a relief, both creatively and commercially, once a more reliable line-up had been finally established.

Bob Siebenberg was quoted in December 2014 in *Modern Drummer* as he elaborated on the positive sense of morale the band had at the time; "The arrangements to these songs are very streamlined and very well thought-out. Rick and Roger were totally absorbed in the process — as we all were — but these were songs they'd been cooking up for quite a while, and they had a pretty good idea how they wanted them to come off. As for the mixing, it was an all-hands-on-deck affair. Everyone had a job to do. All pre-automation, pre-digital — totally handmade."

Roger was quoted in *FM Forecast* in September 1975 regarding how even after having written the songs that would later be used on *Crime Of The Century*, they had sat unused for so long because it wasn't felt that the band had the right line-up during the days of Supertramp's first two albums; "We'd been waiting to do them (the songs), for the right band to come along and do them, you see, we've had a go at them before with the wrong band and if they hadn't worked and if we hadn't done them this time around we would never have done them and they were too good to lose really... we were pretty certain these were going to be the tracks so we just plodded on 'til every single one worked. We were in the studio for five months and we sweated blood."

John was quoted in the same interview; "We didn't do 'em in the order they're actually done here (on the album). That was juggled so that they all fitted together in such a way that makes good listening going from one track to the other. Basic tracks were done in a coupla' weeks and then there were a coupla' three months adding and experimenting and then the last coupla' months were spent mixing the whole thing down."

Such was the extent to which the first two Supertramp albums paled into obscurity at the time of their *Crime Of The Century* album, that when Pete Makowski wrote about the band in *Sounds* in December 1975, for whatever reason, he only acknowledged the band's existence going as far back as 1973. I suppose he was referring to what came to be known as the classic line-up of Supertramp but it is still fascinating to observe how much the first eponymous album and *Indelibly Stamped* were overlooked at the time; "Two years and two months, that's how long Supertramp have been together believe it or not. Two years and two sensational albums – *Crime Of The Century* and *Crisis? What Crisis?* – Supertramp have carved their name in a market that's literally crying out for quality. That's what the 'Tramp are, a quality band who, with bands like 10cc, set themselves high standards that they continually maintain. Supertramp are Rick Davies (keyboards/vocals), Roger Hodgson (guitar/keyboards/vocals), Dougie Thomson (bass), John Helliwell (saxophone, various instruments) and Bob C. Benberg (drums). But Supertramp have been around for quite a while in various forms, this line-up is the culmination of years of paying dues."

It certainly seems that the pressure had been on for Supertramp in terms of needing the *Crime Of The Century* album to do well. John Helliwell was quoted in *Sounds* in December 1975; "Well with A&M helping us out because we couldn't work, it worked out that we'd have to sell three quarters of a million copies to break even, so we'll be getting there soon enough."

In the same interview, Rick Davies added that the sales of the album were "nearly there already" by then. Roger was quoted in *Melody Maker* in January 1975 as he considered how far Supertramp had come with their new (and indeed stable) line-up, as featured on *Crime Of The Century*; "We (Hodgson and Davies) were thinking of just forgetting it when fate stepped in and said 'Okay, you can have it, you can have anything you want'... We found Bob (Siebenberg) and he was just the drummer we were looking for, for ages. Dougie had joined by that time and he knew John and he was just unbelievable as a sax player and he fitted in well. Everything's gone well from then."

In the same article, Hodgson was quoted as he spoke highly of Supertramp as a band; "There's no weakness in the band. If any one of the band left it would be nigh on

SUPER DUPER 'TRAMP

A TRIPLE measure of Supertramp in a little over twenty-four hours is a pretty heady experience. They, alas, will tread one of two paths — the lonely to obscurity or the gilt-edged to recognition.

The latter way is nothing more than they deserve. For Supertramp is a band for connoiseurs and right-minded people; a lovely combination of innovation and fresh tingle.

I'm not sure they were at all fully appreciated at gigs in Plymouth or Torquay on successive nights. The telly provided a third fill — as though to reaffirm their consistency — when the "Whistle Test" featured them.

Plymouth was a revelation. Utilising a huge backdrop to a spotlight flooded stage, Supertramp were superduper playing near everything from "Crime Of The Century". It was a date that gelled like peaches and cream — much to do with the use of four keyboards — ordinary and electric pianos, an organ and a string machine that was beautiful as a kind of refined mellotron.

The band — Richard Davies (vocals and keyboards), Roger Hodgson (vocals, guitar, pianos), John Harriwell (saxophones, clarinets), Doug Thompson (bass) and drummer Bob Benberg — relied exclusively on an eloquence and elegance so sadly missing in this mishapen electronic age. They did "Dreamer", the new single, "Rudy" and lots more from "Crime".

After being off the road for an infinitely long time, it is good to welcome Supertramp back.

Supporting them was the excellent Steve Ashley and a more-superior film of Mike Oldfield's "Tubular Bells". — DAVID HARRIS

Supertramp: the great crusade

THIS IS your chance to learn how to improve yourself and get on in the world as a member of a rock group. This is no easy recipe we give to friends, but a tale of hardship, disappointment, trivial relations, yet the end of SUCCESS, of FAME. Being interviewed for SOUNDS. In a way you will learn how a small and struggling band called Supertramp, loved and admired by the likes of John Peel and by Alan Freeman, find the road to true happiness, and become SUPERTRAMP, loved and admired by the likes of Alan Freeman, John Peel and others . . . YES! . . . thousands

We take you back to the very beginning, to the days when a burning ambition was kindled in the hearts of our young heroes, a will to succeed despite everything. We talk to two of Supertramp's greatest admirers, keyboard player Roger Hodgson, one of two singers and singers. We learn from them the joys of becoming part of a happy, optimistic band, setting out on the road to success. What glorious days they were, or so Roger (for we may call him that) puts it, "When I joined this group I

The band had gone from success to success, they had played as support to Ten Years After and been spotted by your writer as a bright Hope. They had played in huge auditoriums, none greater than the upstairs rooms of pubs and clubs, where they enthralled handfuls of people at a time. Roger remembers the hightop of it all, a tour of Norway, and tells as every detail, "It almost finished, it was unbelievable. It was so traumatic experience, a very traumatic experience. We were thinking of calling it a day," They sold money, everything, even sold their equipment to keep going.

But this is no ordinary story. These boys had courage. They combined. They squired new players to replace those who could not stand the pace. They mended their ways and decided to try to lose money. Their co-writers,

was shocked, the shambles it was in, shocked I was. Everything was in a shambles, the business side of it, the musical side of it, the whole thing was just chaos." How romantically our young Scotsman recalls those early days.

A fairy godmother had been watching them all these years. She saw that the music was good, and allowed it into the charts. This was the start for the first time the band had real debts they could play to a thousand delighted people at a time, be a headline band and lose big money. This was the goal they had aimed for; they had met their motto, "with their motto." Half the mystery, now knowing. The killer of life is comfort. It turns you into a vegetable.",

This the band would never be. Each time disaster loomed in the form of rewards, they found new ways to avoid it. They spent minutes, hours, years rehearsing, refining, hours music. Decades of studio time had perfected every sound. They ensured they would never be rich. Their stage equipment,

Hodgson and Rick Davies, own years penning beautiful music that would not be commercial. They put together a master work, "Crime Of The Century" and waited for it to flop.

But it was a flop, their light crew, their entourage, everything was designed to take money from the boys' pockets and give it to the poor, the needy, the deserving pop fans.

The word spread. People who had found such ridiculous value for money. "How can they do it at the price?" they told their friends. "Thousands flocked to their concerts. "It's such a bargain!" The exquisite beauty of the record shocked many of the like Genesis. It's like Pink Floyd, it's like Elton John. It's wonderful.

Who could say where this story might end? The great crusade, the mighty Supertramp itself, would there be no end to their generosity, always starve? Would their depths of despair might be dead, to drone greater and greater music from their hearts? Only time can tell us the one thing is certain, the answer to the questions world will never be the same again. — HOWARD FIELD, ING.

impossible to replace them really. There are so many sides to Supertramp it's unbelievable. *Crime Of The Century* is one side, the drama side, but there's so much humour in the band I think we'll probably get that coming out on stage eventually."

With Supertramp having been predominantly a nameless band in terms of characters and personalities (at least in terms of the media), it was the success of *Crime Of The Century* that resulted in the media taking more interest. As it was reported in *Melody Maker* in January 1975, "Supertramp is not a new name and yet, until the chart success of their third album, few people had heard of them. Their first album, Supertramp, was well received critically but (as Rick Davies was quoted) 'it didn't do much from a sales point of view', the second, *Indelibly Stamped*, sank almost without trace and the band turned with, perhaps a hint of desperation, to *Crime*. By the time this was being recorded, Supertramp was made up of four of the five present members – and drummer Bob Benberg was added while recording was in progress. Now the 'Tramp is in a healthy position. The band completed their first headlining tour towards the end of last year, capitalising on the success of *Crime Of The Century*, and now they stand poised to consolidate that success with another British tour, to kick off this month. In addition, Supertramp have their sights set on the States where *Crime Of The Century* enjoyed several regional chart breakouts just after Christmas. A&M, their record company, have a selective tour scheduled for this year. And finally, Europe comes into the scheme of things for Supertramp as well. A tour and heavy promotion by the record company are in the offing. All this must be intensely gratifying for a band which, at times, has been close to breaking up on several occasions."

In February 1975, *Record Mirror* advocated; "It's highly likely that Supertramp will have a big impact on both the single and album charts and if they don't, that will surely be the crime of the century." Well, as good fortune and hard work would have it, *Crime Of The Century*, Supertramp's third studio album, marked their commercial breakthrough in both the UK and the US.

The album was released in September 1974 on A&M Records. Single releases from the album also had success, particularly 'Dreamer' in the UK and 'Bloody Well Right' in the US. *Crime Of The Century* was a top ten album in the UK and a top forty album in the US prior to eventually being certified gold there in 1977 after the release of their later album, *Even In The Quietest Moments…*

Although Stanley August Miesegaes had withdrawn financial support in 1972 after *Indelibly Stamped* was a commercial flop in 1971, the liner notes on *Crime Of The Century* pay homage to him with the simply stated, "To Sam". On the 2014 re-mastered release of the album, the liner notes contain some fascinating insights into the writing of some of the songs. Of the song, 'Hide In Your Shell', Hodgson was quoted; "I was twenty three when I wrote that song, confused about life and like a lot of people are at that age, trying to hide my insecurities. I've always been able to express my innermost feelings more openly in song and 'Hide in Your Shell' came to me at a time when I was feeling very lonely — lonely both in life and within the band — with no one who shared my spiritual quest."

As Hodgson was quoted in *Goldmine* in November 2007, "'Hide In Your Shell' is very much, you know, hide away from the world because it's too painful to expose yourself. My experiences are not just unique to me, a lot of people experience what I feel, or what I've felt, and what I've expressed in my songs, and I think a lot of people have found comfort in that, that they're not alone."

The liner notes also tell of how 'Dreamer' was composed by Hodgson at his mother's house on his Wurlitzer piano. He was quoted; "I was excited — it was the first time I laid hands on a Wurlitzer." He was just nineteen when he wrote the song. 'If Everyone Was Listening' was inspired by Shakespeare's *As You Like It* adage ("All the world's a stage, and all the men are merely players.").

The success of *Crime Of The Century* was such that the media were beginning to take greater interest in the band dynamics within Supertramp. In *New Musical Express* in February 1975, the journalist offered an interesting insight into the rapport between Hodgson and Davies at the time of such interview; "*Crime Of The Century* is Supertramp's own sardonic, and at times downright derisive, brand of existentialism. Accordingly one would expect its two main creators to at least be a little contemptuous of life. One might even be unsurprised were they to launch into entertaining invective, not to speak of outright cynicism. But Richard Davies and Roger Hodgson are not a bit like that. Davies is a stolid, laconic individual, prone to long bouts of silence, and obviously bemused by the current interest Supertramp are creating with their chart success. Hodgson, by comparison, is garrulous, bright and helpful in manner — though he, too, is pretty non-committal, especially when discussing the band's music. But if they decided to become a pair of comedians one suspects Davies would be the strong, silent type, and Hodgson his eager-to-please sidekick. They'd be a wow with a routine."

That all sounds very entertaining! However, when it came to the duo being willing to offer more information on band dynamics and commercial ambitions, they were seemingly less exuberant. As the journalist surmised, "As it is, they have no routine at all and this particular interview was the proverbial blood-out-of-a-stone job. No matter." In the same feature in *New Musical Express*, the journalist offered an interesting take on Supertramp's stage presence; "On stage, though, the situation is somewhat different — as Supertramp's successful opener to their current tour at Sheffield City Hall illustrated. There it's perfectly fine to look a shade mean 'n' moody, and of course there are the other visual (not to mention musical) distractions, notably chirpy saxophonist John Anthony Helliwell smacking his lips together so that they sink into his face like he'd forgotten to slip his dentures in. Towards the back of the stage there's the wasted-looking and slightly dour Scots bassist Dougie Thomson, who sways in time to the music like a cork floating gracefully on water. To his right, the short-haired, reserved American drummer, Bob C. Benberg. Musically their act — based to a great extent on the *Crime Of The Century* album — is excellent. Although they have an introverted image, they pace their set smoothly, running through a multitude of instrument changes, as they steadily gain momentum, eventually attaining a suitably climatic conclusion with the title track of the LP."

In an interview with *Modern Drummer* in December 2014, Bob Siebenberg considered that Supertramp was at its artistic peak during the making of the *Crime Of The Century* album. There was certainly a lot of creativity to it. The train sound in the song 'Rudy' was recorded at Paddington Station in London whilst the crowd noises in the song were recorded at Leicester Square.

Although *Crime Of The Century* deals with themes of mental health and loneliness, it was generally considered by the band that it is not a concept album and that any thread or common theme is up to the listener's perception. For the creation of the album's cover, artist Paul Wakefield was working on his first assignment; he was new to doing album covers but was established as an artist. A&M's art director at the time, Fabio Nicoli, invited him to the studio where Supertramp were recording. Wakefield read the lyrics as a starting point from which to construct some imagery for the artwork. His initial ideas for the cover included a teddy bear that had been stabbed in an alleyway with all its blood and guts spilling out all over the place. Yep, that's what the artist got from the lyrics! Dark but when you consider the themes of loneliness and alienation on the album, it is understandable. The violence of this idea though, was such that inevitably, A&M put this idea of Wakefield's on the "no" pile.

Eventually, Wakefield began to explore ideas in the lexicon of prison and entrapment which is what ultimately led to the album cover being what it is. A friend of the artist made a set of polished aluminum bars. They were welded to a stand so that Wakefield's twin brother, whose hands were whitened with stage makeup, could grab the bars. Using multiple exposures on the camera, a number of photos were shot on transparent film. They were combined with a backlit image of the night sky (which was actually a black card sheet with holes that had been poked into it).

Hodgson considered the material on *Crime Of The Century* to be "the strength" of the band. He was quoted in January 1975 in *Melody Maker*; "It keeps all of us interested and makes fresh demands on us every time we have to do something. I think Bob's playing things now he'd never even dreamt of before. I've been writing songs ever since I was twelve and Rick and I are still writing all the time. The songs on *Crime Of The Century* weren't even our favourites but we recorded them because this was something that had been planned three years before. Most of the songs had been written for that long. They seemed to suit each other for an album so we decided to put it out. The next album's going to be completely different because the songs are completely different. I don't know two of our songs that sound anything like each other... There are so many songs waiting to be recorded it's really difficult to know what to pick."

Although many considered *Crime Of The Century* to be a concept album, Supertramp were keen to assert that it wasn't. Hodgson was quoted in February 1975 in *New Musical Express*; "I tell you what, reviewers have got this album much clearer than we have. We didn't actually realise exactly what we'd done until we heard all the eight songs one after another. When I first heard it I was blown apart. I don't know why... but it does have that effect on you. It means something completely different to me than it means to Rick."

In the same interview, Rick was quoted; "What it means to me is feeling right about everything that's going down at that time you're doing it. That's all it means to me, that the lyrics are right for the song, that the arrangements are right for the song. That the mood's right." As the journalist eloquently surmised, "The two musicians are too close to it (the album) to rationalise its content."

Roger was quoted in *FM Forecast* in September 1975; "It really isn't a concept album, I must explain that. It's just a series of ideas strung together so that they sound in logical order and they take the listener through a journey of his own emotions and thoughts really, it's like a thought provoker rather than a concept. I mean, if you ask all five of us individually what the album's about, you'll get five different replies."

Whilst *Crime Of The Century* isn't a concept album, as Hodgson was quoted in February 1975 in *New Musical Express*, "I think we could tell you what each song is about. As a concept, which wasn't particularly planned, I think the reason it's taken off is half the music and half the sign of the times, really. *Crime Of The Century* really does go with what's happening in the world today."

Roger Hodgson has often been candid in interviews about how he has had so many unanswered questions and felt alienated from a young age. He was quoted in *Classic Rock Revisited* in February 2012; "I was very sensitive and intuitive. I don't know whether I felt different but I had very deep questions going on and I was surprised that other people didn't. I wanted to know where true happiness lay. I wanted to know who or what God was because it didn't make any sense. The God they taught me was not working. I knew there had to be an inward connection as that is where everything was pointing. It was a connection that was severely lacking in me and I was longing for it."

Roger was quoted in *Record Mirror* in March 1975; "When the album came out we had no thoughts of a single but we knew that if there was going to be a single then 'Dreamer' would be it. It was simply the most commercial track on the album. We couldn't go out and pen a single. We don't write like that. Neither Rick nor I can sit down and write a song just like that. Some days you wake up and you've got an idea. Then you can go for two months without one and 'Dreamer' was exactly like that. It came out on record just as I first recorded it on my home tape. The final single was near enough unchanged too. The single success hasn't hit us at all really. We're obviously interested in it but it hasn't effected us any since it happened. Supertramp doesn't feel like a singles band now and we don't relate to the Cassidys, or whoever. We're only the same as they are from the point of view that we both release records. *Top Of The Pops* is one of about two programmes which appeals to people who buy singles. So we did it but the biggest problem is that it's not geared to rock 'n' roll. We did *Top Of The Pops* once before when we appeared as Gilbert O'Sullivan's backing band, and I remember thinking then that it was a joke. But at least the people were enjoying themselves. This time the vibe of the whole thing was so cold, and it's not the kids' fault, they thought it was a joke."

I think it's important to point out here that Hodgson probably wasn't being disparaging of *Top Of The Pops*. In the same interview he elaborated on the clinical nature of the process and how it was essentially about marketing and not music. In the same interview, Dougie added; "It was one of those things. We had the chance of doing it so we quickly got the backing track together. Then we go out there, not terribly geared to doing the show and there's nothing to get off on. We need something, but there was nothing."

Crime Of The Century was Supertramp's first top forty album in the US. It also signified the band's breakthrough in the UK where it peaked at number four in the albums chart in March 1975 and 'Dreamer' got to number thirteen in the singles chart in the same month. Additionally, *Crime Of The Century* was the album that saw Supertramp crack the Canadian market; the album stayed in the charts there for over two years, during which period it sold over a million copies. Many of the songs from the album were consistently used in the band's live sets throughout their performing career, in particular, 'School', 'Dreamer', 'Bloody Well Right', Rudy' and the album's title song. Hodgson was quoted in *The San Diego Union Tribune* in February 2011; "'Dreamer' is such fun to perform — and automatically lifts people's spirits. It's a "good medicine" song."

Pete Makowski reported in *Sounds* in December 1975 on what the classic line-up of Supertramp's first gig was like; "The first time Supertramp played together in their current format was a gig in Jersey for a Lord's party. A friend of a friend, of a friend job." In the same article, Bob Siebenberg was quoted; "I got so drunk I couldn't play so I spent the whole of the break sobering up and by that time the rest of the band got so drunk they couldn't play!" First time nerves perhaps? Overexcitement? Who knows!

But Supertramp's first live performance of *Crime Of The Century* was still quite primitive too. It was at an A&M gathering in the Kings Road Theatre. John Helliwell was quoted in the same feature; "There were so many things happening backstage you just wouldn't have believed it." Rick Davies added, "We never worked with a full lighting crew so when they went out we couldn't see a thing. And I remembered on one particular number I had to open in complete darkness, I couldn't see anything so I couldn't play, which meant the lights wouldn't go on. We really bluffed through it and hoped for the best."

It wasn't that long after that the band toured Britain, Europe and America. Such was the acceleration of their success. The stage show that accompanied the *Crime Of The Century* album certainly required a lot of thought, co-ordination and frankly, clever thinking when it came to ergonomics. As Rick Davies was quoted in *Beat Instrumental* in April 1975; "It's getting to be routine now playing all those instruments on stage, but it was a bit difficult. It's not difficult for me, it's just a question of whether it's going to upset people seeing so much movement, but I think if we get it smooth, which I think it is now, it's okay."

In the same feature, when the interviewer alluded to the idea that Davies' "dashing about can sometimes remind the viewer of Rick Wakeman's on stage antics", Davies' reply was, "No way am I going to do a Wakeman, absolutely not. I've got very little technique in that sense, I won't even start thinking about a solo album for a while. I will do when we've got three hit albums and we can sit back and think."

As was explained by the journalist in the same article; "On stage with Supertramp, founder member Richard Davies plays Wurlitzer piano, Hammond 102 organ, grand piano and harmonica. His equipment is completed by two Leslies. Which all sounds very grand, but when there are five musicians sharing the platform things can get a bit hectic. Now that Supertramp have cracked it they're working a lot more and it wasn't until recently that Richard stopped worrying about having to dash from instrument to instrument during a set."

Dougie Thomson was quoted in *Record Mirror* in March 1975; "Whatever or whenever we change, we'll make sure that what we put in is more substantial than what we take out. What we found with *Crime Of The Century* was that once we played it live, the songs started to live. The album was very correct. That was a collection of songs that we thought would work as a collection of songs, but it took the band a long time to cope with the thing as an entity. But I think we've performed the last live gig with *Crime Of The Century* as the basis, we'll start pulling out numbers now."

In the same feature, Roger Hodgson was quoted; "One of the helpful things with *Crime Of The Century* was that reviewers knew nothing or little about Supertramp beforehand and so met the album with an open mind. Next time, now that they've built us up as the new find, they'll want to pull us down. And whatever we put out, the first thing they're going to do is compare it with *Crime Of The Century*."

Crime Of The Century was ultimately the album that Supertramp needed in order for the continuation of the band to be possible. It certainly achieved that although, there were greater highs to come. As Roger Hodgson was quoted at the time of the album's success in February 1975 in *New Musical Express*; "It's a great band, it's got a load of potential. How much of that potential is allowed to get out, only time will tell."

Although mono releases had given way to stereo by the late sixties it was still commonplace in America to release singles for radio play with the one track in both mono and stereo as AM radio stations broadcasted in mono.

A relatively early shot of "The established line-up". From left: Rick Davies, Dougie Thomson, John Helliwell, Roger Hodgson & Bob Siebenberg.

SUPERTRAMP

ON TOUR
PERFORMING
CRIME OF THE CENTURY

23rd October GUILDFORD CIVIC HALL
25th October OLD BIRMINGHAM REP THEATRE
26th October COLLEGIATE THEATRE LONDON
31st October ST. ANDREWS UNIVERSITY
1st November ABERDEEN UNIVERSITY
2nd November DUNDEE UNIVERSITY
5th November BRADFORD UNIVERSITY
6th November MANCHESTER UNIVERSITY
8th November LAMPETER UNIVERSITY
9th November BANGOR UNIVERSITY
12th November QUEENS THEATRE BURSLEM, STOKE
15th November NORTH STAFFS. POLY.

Chapter Five:
Crisis? What Crisis? (1975)

Crisis? What Crisis? (1975)

Rick Davies – keyboards,
harmonica, lead and
backing vocals
Roger Hodgson – electric
and acoustic guitars,
keyboards flageolet, cello,
marimba, electric sitar, lead
and backing vocals
John Helliwell –
saxophones, clarinet and
bass clarinet, backing vocals
Dougie Thomson – bass
guitar
Bob C. Benberg – drums

Side one
1. Easy Does It
2. Sister Moonshine
3. Ain't Nobody But Me
4. A Soapbox Opera
5. Another Man's Woman

Side two
6. Lady
7. Poor Boy
8. Just A Normal Day
9. The Meaning
10. Two Of Us

*C*risis? What Crisis? was the first of
Supertramp's albums to be recorded
in America. The sessions for the album
took place at London's Ramport Studios and
Scorpio Studios as well as A&M Studios in
Los Angeles. After the success of *Crime Of
The Century*, the pressure was on for the band
to offer something that met high expectations.
The stress of the situation was possibly
exemplified by the fact that A&M insisted that
work on what would become Supertramp's
fourth studio album, began straight after the
tour for *Crime Of The Century*. Much like with
the band's second album, *Indelibly Stamped*,
writing and rehearsal time was minimal and
Crisis? What Crisis? was perhaps a labour of
obligation rather than a labour of love for the

band. Such was the rushed approach to *Crisis? What Crisis?* that production had to be paused at one point in order that Hodgson and Davies could write more material for it. One such song that came out of the situation was 'Ain't Nobody But Me'. It is interesting to consider that by this point in their writing partnership, Hodgson and Davies would have had plenty of material to fall back on as a result of the many songs that didn't make it onto the *Crime Of The Century* album. However, for whatever reason, new material was required and as a result, *Crisis? What Crisis?* was seemingly not given the time and energy it needed in order to reach its full potential. That said, four of the album's songs, 'Sister Moonshine', 'Another Man's Woman', 'Lady' and 'Just A Normal Day', were all performed in the live sets prior to recording the album. On balance, although there was clearly an element of things feeling rushed, Supertramp's fourth album is not without worthwhile and indeed good, material.

After the success of *Crime Of The Century*, Davies was quoted in *Sounds* in December 1975 as he expressed his concerns about how *Crisis? What Crisis?* may be received in the press; "I expected a slightly harder time with the album, opposite to what I initially thought, I expected it to be good for *Crime Of The Century* and not for this one. But the press are funny, there's only a few people that you've got confidence in as far as what they think and sooner or later they blow it for you by saying something completely silly."

In the same article, Davies was quoted as he addressed a question about the fact that *Crisis? What Crisis?* had made use of material that hadn't made it onto the *Crime Of The Century* album; "There hasn't been a great spate of writing, certainly not from me, I think Roger has done a bit more." Dougie added; "It seems easier for Roger as he only needs a guitar, while Rick needs to be locked away somewhere with a piano."

The band were very candid in this interview about the fact that *Crisis? What Crisis?* hadn't really been given the time it needed to emerge as a good album. Davies was quoted; "We need a break, where we can get fresh ideas", to which Dougie added, "We never stopped, and it will have been two years solid work by the time we do stop. The important thing is that the music stays good. If it needs to stop — and thinking about — then that's what's going to happen!"

It is possible that the theme of not having the time that they really wanted would remain typical throughout Supertramp's tenure. Even during the time of their albums that followed *Crisis? What Crisis?*, the band alluded to this being a problem. Rick was quoted in *New Musical Express* in August 1977; "I'd like to do more but this is all down to our touring schedule and working out time for writing and recording. It's up to the whole band to sort that out. There's a lot of things in the works and everybody's trying to think out and discuss a policy for the future."

Roger Hodgson was quoted in November 2007 in *Goldmine*; "*Crisis? What Crisis?*… There was a lot of pressure to come up with an album quickly and go out on tour after the success of *Crime Of The Century*, so there was a lot of pressure on that one. I knew we had the songs. I think *Crisis? What Crisis* is a great selection of songs, but they

didn't come out as good as I was hoping, anyway. And part of that was just the stressful situation we were under, so yes, the title of that album definitely suited what was going on with the band. In fact, it came from a sketch that Rick did in the waiting room of the studio, and it reflected the stress we were under in just getting that album completed."

It certainly seems that even without hindsight, Supertramp may have been feeling quite pressured to write songs for the album that followed the busy whirlwind they experienced from *Crime Of The Century*. During the time of the *Crime Of The Century* tour, Hodgson was quoted in *FM Forecast* in September 1975; "We haven't had a chance to write at all, it's mostly at home that we've written. I live in the country at home so that gives me a lot of time. Actually, hotel rooms generally, if you get the time, like if you're in a place for a couple of days, they're a good place to write. You haven't got any attachments around you, you haven't got any friends or relatives or dogs to distract you. It's great, I really enjoy writing in hotel rooms. This tour's pretty hectic so I haven't had a chance - just playing, Holiday Inn, gig, Holiday Inn, playing."

Rick Davies was quoted in *Beat Instrumental* in April 1975; "I went home at Christmas (1974) specifically to try and write but it didn't happen. There's lots of stuff in the can but I want to know what's going to come out of me next and I'm a little bit short on ego about that. We're thinking about the format of the next album. The approach is really the most important thing because if you have a successful album out, as we're now finding out, it's putting a certain amount of crunch on you as you're gonna be disappointed if the next one's not going to do something as well."

It really comes across that there was a lot of pressure on the band to come up with the goods, both amongst themselves and in terms of communicating to the media at the time that everything was all going well. *Cash Box* reported in May 1975; "Supertramp have released the probably most talked about, impressive LP in recent days for A&M and have an orchestrated, polyrhythmic and highly intelligent approach to their music that should feature prominently in their future success. Already veterans of two British tours and one recent swing through the US, the band tells *Cash Box* that they have an abundance of material already in the can for the next LP. We can't wait!"

The comparison between how *Crisis? What Crisis?* was made compared to *Crime Of The Century* was noted well by a journalist in *Sounds* in May 1976; "For *Crime Of The Century*, material was rehearsed before actual studio time was bought (the live show was constructed after the album was completed) and consequently the feel embodies a cohesiveness and punchiness. But on *Crisis? What Crisis?* the band entered the studio following a tour and had no real indication of any direction."

Rick Davies was quoted in the same *Sounds* feature; "*Crisis? What Crisis?* was done pretty much right off the road and we don't feel it was quite as successful as it should have been. But that was a chance we had to take. It got lost in the end, and it took us a long time to get the right feel."

Crisis? What Crisis? wasn't a concept album but there is a certainly an interesting theme present, as is alluded to on the album's cover art which features a man enjoying the haven of life in a deckchair under an umbrella whilst all around him is chaos and disarray. As with Supertramp's previous album, artist Paul Wakefield made the cover art for *Crisis? What Crisis?*. He photographed images of the Welsh mining valleys. The image of the model was shot in the studio and was added to the background image afterwards.

By the time of the *Crisis? What Crisis?* album, Supertramp were taking live gigs in their stride. Rick Davies was quoted in *Sounds* in December 1975; "I think it's taken almost this long to get completely on top of it without worrying about little knobs and switches, so in a way you can go out there and relax. There's only a couple of numbers that worry me technically. Once you start getting on top of it, that's when you have to be careful that you're not going to become complacent. When you stop thinking 'is it going to be alright?' and start thinking 'this is going to be a piece of piss' — it's only on the last gigs that I've thought this is nothing, I can do this easy, but you soon get brought down to earth about it all."

Bob Siebenberg was quoted in *Melody Maker* in November 1975; "We aim to reproduce as closely as possible the sound we produce on stage to the record. I think we do pretty well… In Glasgow on the last tour, all the girls sang along with Roger on the opening verse of 'If Everyone Was Listening'. It really gives you a shiver."

Supertramp's performance at Santa Monica Civic was reviewed in *Cash Box* in April 1976; "From the moment the harmonica riff began on 'School', the mounting tension and energy of the audience exploded into a frenzy. The rest of the evening was one big ball of energy with good times and good vibes for all. Supertramp are hot. Each time the band struck the first chord to a new number the crowd already knew what the tune was and began to party. Supertramp does not get into flashy lighting and gimmicks. Their musicianship was so brilliant and developed to such a high degree that really nothing else was needed. Every number was impeccable from start to finish. 'Bloody Well Right', 'Sister Moonshine', 'Lady', 'Dreamer', 'Rudy', 'Ain't Nobody But Me' and 'Hide In Your Shell' were just a few of the selections that helped create the electronic symphony that was happening inside the arena. They closed their extraordinary show with 'Crime Of The Century', complete with chilling projection on screen. Supertramp should definitely be rated as one of the finest bands produced in the seventies world of rock."

Bob Siebenberg was quoted in *Melody Maker* in November 1975; "We played to 30,000 on the last tour and by the time we've finished this one we'll have played in front of maybe twice that number. We've been selling out these concerts with very little advertising, no posters around the gigs before the shows and no new album — it only came out this week, I find it incredible. I guess I don't really know who our fans are. Some older people, a few little kids. We're hitting everybody in some way or other. 'Dreamer' brought in the younger ones."

Record Mirror included *Crisis? What Crisis?* in its list of notable albums for 1975. The album was certainly one that received mixed reviews though; It was reviewed in *Melody Maker* in November 1975; "Well might Supertramp demand what crisis. During

a year in which we are repeatedly being informed of all the depths of our despair, Supertramp have become giant killers. Reaching the top of *Melody Maker's* album chart with *Crime Of The Century* was surprising, for it was pleasant but unremarkable. Their follow up is even more pleasant but equally unremarkable. It has the feeling of an embryonic Pink Floyd, with brief bouts of foot-tapping. They stick in the same lazy groove throughout, but in a quietly infectious way, it's warming and enjoyable. They may not be trying anything too ambitious but they perform in a highly professional style, while Ken Scott's production is at times impeccable. While there's a substantial use of keyboards (and it's refreshing to hear extensive use of piano as opposed to synthesiser), they steer clear of the overblown production of many beloved Pomp Rock kings. The singing shared by Roger Hodgson and Rick Davies, also responsible for all the material, is never very exciting but the atmosphere of the record is unsuited to a Jagger or Daltrey. They harmonise neatly, while backing voices are used with much intelligence, and arrangements complement the pensive mood. What the hell if there are times when you feel you want to grab them by the necks and shake them out of their melancholy. The first side is vastly better than the second, which occasionally shows the danger signs of drifting into monotony. 'Easy Does It', a gentle melodic, unaccompanied number, is an attractive opener that's quite representative of what follows. Its immediate successor, 'Sister Moonshine', is one of the most interesting (and liveliest) tracks, both lyrically and musically. Not too dissimilar to 'Dreamer', it's the nearest they come to displaying a real emotion other than melancholy and the song is beautifully constructed, with driving harmonica rhythms at the end delightfully rounding it off. This and not the dirge-like 'Lady' which appears on the second side, should be the single. 'Ain't Nobody But Me' is forgettable until it's kicked into life by a marvellous outbreak of brass in the middle, which makes it undeniable that it's the arrangements, so clean and absorbing, that hold you when all else threatens to flag. 'A Soapbox Opera' sees them a little out of their depth, moving into territory governed by 10cc with a 'One Night In Paris' type interlude that rails against the clergy. The churchy effects and the incorporation of a lone voice singing 'All Things Bright And Beautiful' is faintly pretentious, but the whole thing is retrieved by a compelling hook-line and chorus. The second side tends to be dour but it does include 'Poor Boy', the most free-ranging track on the album, which even begins to swing slightly, suggesting there's a side to Supertramp we haven't yet seen and includes a glorious clarinet solo. Lyrically too — it's anthem to the working class — it stands up better than the other tracks. Praise for the album as a whole is not unstinted. It's all too inhibited and claustrophobic. But Supertramp can certainly write tunes that stick in the mind, even though they do not bear too much probing."

Crikey! That's quite a linguistically expressive review isn't it! As in, whoever wrote it seems to have been pretty poetic with their use of language. If the reviewer was using just one phoneme to describe his opinion of the album, I guess the best choice would have been "meh". As the reviewer captions a photograph from one of the live shows, "Supertramp: unremarkable". With the reviewer not having much of a positive opinion of the *Crime Of The Century* album, it's possible that they simply just weren't a Supertramp fan.

The album was panned by *Rolling Stone* in January 1976; "Supertramp, whose *Crime Of The Century* was a surprise hit of 1975, are back with a neatly timed follow up, *Crisis? What Crisis?* (with suitably heady cover — a man sunbathing amid rubbish while rain falls and smokestacks blow pollution into already ominously gray skies). The biggest crisis is trying to get through both sides of this record. Supertramp is led by guitarist Roger Hodgson and keyboard player Richard Davies who are responsible (as in guilty) for all the group's words and music. Most of their lyrics are vignettes depicting the loss of communication among people and the absence of moral values in today's world, leading to such stimulating conclusions as this complex couplet from 'Just A Normal Day': 'Eat a lot, sleep a lot/Passing the time of day/Maybe I'll find my way.' The band carries off the amazing trick of stretching three and four minute songs into five and six minute affairs with unison repetition of themes instead of solos. There's even one song ('Two Of Us') that seems profoundly influenced by post-Apple George Harrison."

What a harsh review! Especially the comment about getting through the whole record being the biggest crisis! I'm not simply saying it's a harsh review because I like Supertramp, I'm saying that it's a harsh review on the basis that the album is not without its merits, both musically and in terms of depicting an interesting period in the band's discography. Such is the way that the album was perceived by some at the time though

I guess. Besides, when *Crisis? What Crisis?* was released in September 1975, it got into the UK top twenty and the US top fifty. The fact that the singles were commercial flops did not prevent the album itself from having some success. Also, words like "success" and "flop" are so relative aren't they as in yes, *Crisis? What Crisis?* wasn't as big a deal as *Crime Of The Century* but equally, it wasn't a complete failure either. It's all relative really. As Hodgson was quoted in the *St Louis Post Dispatch* in May 1998; "Crime Of The Century* was viewed as a sonic masterpiece and we fell into the trap of thinking 'boy we've got to live up to that now' and it's taken me a long time to realise you've just got to enjoy it the best you can and then move on. Life's too short."

Not everyone was that pleased with *Crisis? What Crisis?*, even Supertramp themselves! Hodgson was quoted in *Billboard* in December 1980; "It didn't turn out as well as we thought. It was a lesson well learned. We only had a month to prepare." Helliwell was quoted in *Record Mirror* in April 1977; "With *Crisis? What Crisis?* we rushed into it, rather in the wake of *Crime Of The Century*." That's not to say though, that the whole thing was a complete and utter flop in every possible regard. The fact is that many people liked it and there were achievements and reviews that reflect that. As was reported in *Cash Box* in April 1976, "Supertramp was congratulated at a luncheon in their honour by A&M records following their three sold out Santa Monica Civic concerts." Now granted, the live shows were using a lot of material from *Crime Of The Century* at the time but still, a sold out show is a sold out show. Besides, the single, 'Lady', was reviewed in *Cash Box* in February 1976; "This single is from the group's *Crisis? What Crisis?* LP and proves without a doubt that there will be no crisis with this band. Tight is not even the word for this calypso tinged rock 'n' roller — each member seems to be keeping a close watch on everything that's happening, they're reading each other's minds. Already receiving FM airplay, this tune will skip more than a few rungs of the pop ladder."

Essentially, I think it's important to point out here that predominantly, the well ploughed narrative is that *Crisis? What Crisis?* was a flop. However, with Supertramp being so popular globally and particularly in Canada, the album was better received in some places than others and to quite a notable extent. In June 1977, it was reported in *Record Mirror*; "Crisis? What Crisis? tops the 200,000 (sales) mark." *Record Mirror & Disc* reviewed *Crisis? What Crisis?* in December 1975; "(It) isn't an album that hits you first time around, but rather gets under your skin the more you play it. Around the fifth time you then realise just how much blood, sweat and elbow grease has gone into the works. Roger Hodgson and Richard Davies have produced some fine songs like 'Sister Moonshine' and 'Another Man's Woman' and the musicianship is of the highest degree. If taken on an overall marking of star quality, content and presentation on *Crisis? What Crisis?* beats *Crime Of The Century* in a photo finish."

It's so important to be open to the subjectivity of how good any music is. At first I was surprised to see a review that praised *Crisis? What Crisis?* as being better than *Crime Of The Century* but having given it some thought, the review makes some valid points about what are enjoyable qualities of *Crisis? What Crisis?*. Just because Supertramp weren't too pleased with the album and just because commercially, it wasn't what *Crime Of The Century* was, it doesn't mean that it was without its merits. Besides, whilst Supertramp may have been disappointed with *Crisis? What Crisis?*, it still climbed its way up the American chart.

© Pictorial Press Ltd / Alamy Stock Photo

Hammersmith Odeon, 1975.

© Laurens van Houten (Frank White Photo Agency)

71

Supertramp

WITH SPECIAL GUEST

FRIDAY, MARCH 19, 1976 8 PM
SEATTLE CENTER ARENA

TICKETS AVAILABLE
BON MARCHE AND ALL SUBURBAN OUTLETS
ALL PARA BUDGET TAPES AND RECORDS
RECORD COMPANY/BAINBRIDGE ISLAND
BAY RECORDS AND TAPES/BREMERTON

PRESENTED BY

ALBATROSS
PRODUCTIONS
CO-SPONSORED BY KJR

Dougie Thomson performing in Amsterdam during the Crisis? What Crisis? Tour 1976.

© Laurens van Houten (Frank White Photo Agency)

Chapter Six:
Even In The Quietest
Moments... (1977)

Even In The Quietest Moments... (1977)

Rick Davies – keyboards, lead and backing vocals
Roger Hodgson – guitars, keyboards, lead and backing vocals
John Helliwell – saxophones, clarinet, melodica, keyboards, backing vocals
Dougie Thomson – bass guitar
Bob C. Benberg – drums

Gary Mielke – Oberheim programming

Side one
1. Give A Little Bit
2. Lover Boy
3. Even In The Quietest Moments
4. Downstream

Side two
5. Babaji
6. From Now On
7. Fool's Overture

Even In The Quietest Moments... was released in April 1977. As before, the album itself was more successful than the singles that came from it; it reached number sixteen in America, number twelve in the UK and number one in Canada. It was during this period that the band made a full relocation to Los Angeles. At the time though, there didn't seem to be any certainty about making America a permanent base. As Hodgson was quoted in *Sounds* in April 1977, "We live in a Supertramp bubble. We are each other's friends so it's like the English vibe is still there. LA is a totally crazy place, none of us like living here particularly. We like the weather and that's about it. We haven't found anywhere we want to live really, although I don't think we want to go back to England. I don't personally miss it but some of the others do. If anything, I miss the subtleties of the English."

The recording location wasn't the only significant change at the time. As was reported in the same article in *Sounds*; "Supertramp have taken a big step on the new LP and decided to produce it themselves, jettisoning the services of Ken Scott. That move comes as a reaction to their last release, *Crisis? What Crisis?*". As Roger explained of *Crisis? What Crisis?* to the interviewer, "It came to mean more to us as a title than it did to other people because it was really a crisis album. We learnt how not to make an album, coming right off the road and going into the studio. It could have been much better than *Crime Of The Century* but it wasn't. We had a lot of bad luck in the studio. We really didn't enjoy making it and in the end it was kind of a patch up job. A lot of people liked it but for us it missed."

Sacking Ken didn't seem to be something that was based on personal reasons though. It comes across that it was more about different people having different styles and approaches to the recording process. Hodgson clarified in the same feature; "Working with Ken, we became perfectionists in a way and went overboard on *Crisis? What Crisis?* and became perfectionists technically. Now we are concentrating on getting the feel of a song down. That's why it has taken so long. Some days we don't feel like playing. So we don't play. Now the sound is not quite so clinical, it's more live and definitely much better."

In defense of Ken Scott though, it seems that he was a valued member of the recording process on Supertramp's earlier albums. In *Modern Drummer* in December 2014, Bob Siebenberg was quoted as he described how good it was to work with Scott on *Crime Of The Century*; "Well, to begin with, we were so fortunate to have Ken at the helm. There was and is no one better in the studio as a producer/engineer than Ken. And that's not to take anything away from our good friend and producer/engineer Peter Henderson, who we worked with on several records later in our career, including *Breakfast In America*. But it was a different time and stage in our career with Ken. He was totally absorbed and working hard to create something that would blow people away. He set the tone for what our records had to be for the rest of our career. In the case of 'Asylum' (from the *Crime Of The Century* album), those were the fills I had cooked up in rehearsals and modified ever so slightly in the studio. Ken recorded them and made them sound the way they do. There was always interaction between us in the studio. We were all in this together, and we had respect for one another and were all willing to take direction. Ken included."

At this point, it also feels important to put it out there that whilst Roger Hodgson has been prolific in interviews in expressing his angle on how Supertramp were feeling about things as a band, Hodgson's perspective on things is not necessarily reflective of how others in the band were feeling. As is the case in the December 2014 interview with *Modern Drummer*, it seems that Siebenberg was happy with Ken Scott's work, at least on the *Crime Of The Century* album.

Even In The Quietest Moments… was recorded mostly at Caribou Ranch Studios in Colorado but the overdubs, vocals and mixing was completed at The Record Plant in Los Angeles. There were logistical reasons for this. As Helliwell was quoted in *Record Mirror* in April 1977; "Caribou was fantastic but we could only book it for two months so we finished the album off in LA. At the same time we were in the Record Plant, the Tubes were in another part of the studios. They were a real scream. They go in for a lot of dressing up and using video screens and putting on a huge stage show. With Supertramp, it doesn't really matter where we work, we find our own level. Supertramp is an entity within itself."

In June 1977, *Record Mirror* reported on Supertramp's growing rapport with Canada; "Supertramp seem to have been taken to heart by their Canadian fans judging by the recent Toronto appearances. Their albums are selling faster than flapjacks, the city's FM radio stations are playing the album tracks to death, concert tickets are touted for many Canadian dollars. In short they're the latest phenomenon. But why Canada? And why Supertramp? Canada has never been regarded as much of a rock culture centre. Indeed, the vast country is ignored by many major touring bands." In the article, the reporter considered how a lot of the music in the Canadian pop charts was mostly British or American. Good on Supertramp for appreciating their Canadian fans.

Even In The Quietest Moments… was the first of Supertramp's albums to be engineered by Peter Henderson, who would continue to fulfill such role with the band for their following three albums. *Even In The Quietest Moments…* was Supertramp's first gold selling album in America. The song, 'Fool's Overture' as well as the album's title track were both given a decent amount of airplay on FM radio (Hodgson was quoted in *The San Diego Union Tribune* in February 2011; "'Fool's Overture' is one of my favourite pieces that I've ever written. Three separate pieces of music that I'd had for a few years magically came together one day.").

The single, 'Give A Little Bit' got to number fifteen in America, number twenty nine in the UK and number eight in Canada. The song was written by Hodgson when he was nineteen or twenty and it wasn't until five or six years later that he introduced it to the band for recording. Hodgson was quoted in *Rolling Stone* in February 2012 as he talked about the philosophy behind the song; "I think without knowing it, I had a degree of wisdom anyway in my late teens. There was a lot of confusion too, but 'Give A Little Bit' came from that era. It was the sixties, so love and peace were definitely what was in the public consciousness, if you like. So that was maybe my contribution to that, but I also believed that and I still believe that and the song really has stood the test of time. It's basically saying you don't need to give a lot, give a little bit and show that you care. And if there's ever a time we need to do that, it's now."

He was quoted in February 2011 in the *North County Times*; "Like many of the songs I have written, 'Give A Little Bit' has such a pure, timeless message that is just as relevant today as when I wrote it as a teenager. It's a song that really inspires people to give a little bit, not give a lot, just give a little bit and see how it feels and show that you care. I believe that true happiness comes from giving — giving our love, giving our time, giving a little bit of ourselves in whatever ways we can."

Roger Hodgson was quoted in November 2007 in *Goldmine*; "*Even in the Quietest Moments…* really reflected my spiritual search. I had done a lot of searching in California and done a lot of yoga retreats and meditation retreats, so the mood of that album I think came from those experiences. *Even in the Quietest Moments…* has the feeling of that because of what I was going through in my life."

At the time, Rick and Roger were prone to disagreements about the thematic nature of lyrics. In particular, Davies passionately objected to Hodgson's use of religious connotations in 'Lord Is It Mine'. Davies was quoted in *Melody Maker* in June 1979; "I gave Roger quite a hard time with 'Lord Is It Mine' and he still got his way. He usually does. I want to try and steer him out of that area a bit, if he's not already steering himself out of it, because it's getting into a rut. Despite what he believes in, it will get limiting. In a group situation, you have to bend a bit. Fine if either of us is doing our own thing for a solo, then you're the artist, but in this context the strongest thing must be the group, and I think that that's been proved quite a few times."

The disagreements didn't seem to get out of hand though. Regarding his response to Davies' stance, Hodgson was quoted; "That's good for me. Rick keeps a rein on me getting too way out in that direction… Any spiritual songs that I had should preferably be born out of experience. It's been a good test to my faith all along anyway. It's good having jokes made about you. I mean, we're all weird in our own ways. Every single one of us. The basic thing we've all got is tolerance and that's why we've all kept together. Socially, we haven't got that much in common but we all respect each other's beliefs and lifestyles. There's a very easy going element which makes it all possible."

As journalist Tony Stewart reported in *New Musical Express* in August 1977, "With *Even In the Quietest Moments…*, Hodgson showed he had discovered religion… The weight of the material came from Hodgson and each of his tracks has a religious element. They reflect his search for spiritual purity and guidance, frequently referring to traditional images of Christ and the Crucifixion. On one song, 'Babaji', he implores the spiritual figure to help the band make music."

Roger was quoted in *New Musical Express* in August 1977; "*On Crime Of The Century*, we co-wrote much more and I think that's another reason why that album worked. The reason *Even In The Quietest Moments…* didn't work in the same way was because we have both become much stronger individuals." In such regard, Rick was quoted as he added that ergonomically, it required a different approach to the writing when working together; "It takes a lot more energy to argue a point because of the strength of the individual now. If I look at a song of Roger's and I think it's wrong, I've got to be really one hundred per cent there to fight that. Usually I just don't have the energy to, because I see it blowing up into a huge misunderstanding."

The song 'Lover Boy' was inspired by the advertisements in men's magazines

Whatever happened to Supertramp?

OHN ANTHONY Helliwell gingerly replaces his cup of too-weak Darjeeling tea, finger crooked, and peers opaquely behind dense spectacles.

"Where would you like to bomb most then?"

This peculiar enquiry — presumably prompted by the arrival of an ice-cream *bombe* on the hotel restaurant table — is left in the air as waiters flit around the aisles, quietly pestering, but Helliwell as always tacks firmly on to his line of thought.

"I mean — if you could bomb one place. I hate somewhere enough for that but I really can't remember."

Glug goes the tea and the fruit flan methodically disappears.

"You could probably bomb Indiannapolis."

What happens there, then, I mutter, picking at what professed on the menu to be pike but which turned out to be more akin to squidgy potatoes.

"Not enough really," continues Helliwell, doggedly.

Dougie Thompson sits diagonally opposite Helliwell and sips determinedly on his second glass of milk.

(Dougie is into *health*).

"Gary, Indiana," he offers uncertainly.

"Yeh you could bomb Gary, Indiana," Helliwell asserts. "Terrible place. Looks like the front of the 'Crisis' cover."

Well that's settled, then except for a sudden pacifist surge from Dougie.

"This is sordid. Bombs are nasty, nasty, nasty things."

Thrice nasty. The point is made.

Dougie and John, incidentally, are members of Supertramp. Supertramp are that English band who've been in America for two years trying to Make It. And they sort of have. Like they've sold out two nights at the Toronto Maple Leaf, 14,000 capacity. Foul Empire Pools, more or less.

This, they are at pains to point out, does not mean they're rich. The week before, they played in front of an audience of 700. Then there's the touring costs, and the stage show and the (very) expensive sound system. It takes a while to recoup.

Conversations about blasting locations in the cosmos to oblivion are untypical of Supertramp. They are a very non-bizarre band, notoriously unopinionated in interview, a journalistically bleak let-the-music-speak-for-itself bunch.

Individually they tend towards the bluff and down-to-earth. Moot points about their approach to music tend to be greeted with an "I can see that" or a "We just do what we do".

Their capability for being unforthright at first seems to stretch into insularity. On the first day in Toronto, there's no sign of the band apart from a cursory glimpse in the hotel bar.

On the second day their caution seems to manifest into paranoia as journalists are denied access to backstage and even turfed out of the soundcheck (a step only usually considered necessary by the most hyper-sensitive of bands).

Later that day, resentment recedes when it is revealed that the expulsion was by order of the sound engineer, a perfectionist who uses a potentially dangerous white-noise machine and not through band hostility. What's more, backstage passes are being arranged for the second concert. Well *OK*. With those obstacles removed Supertramp's debut concert at The Maple Leaf Gardens, Toronto, can be appreciated free of a hassle-cluttered viewpoint. (evn if it still is a bit jetlagged).

T REALLY is impressive, and even with the threat of a magnesium flare sticking to the side of your face (they throw them about y'know, a dangerous party alright) it's exciting. All through the warm up act — The

Tim Lott investigates the strange case of the long lost Supertramp

Hometown Band, a classy bunch of locals — the noise from the audience builds and swells, and the frisbees slice the light and the gargantuan rainbow balloons lumber about aimlessly.

In the cramped, uncomfortable chair rows loud voices throb with impatience. Then down lights, mouths roar, and the band are on.

I think at this point I develop reservations. The set is undeniable and professional fun/art/sophistication or whatever but it keeps stumbling across muddy passages of mediocrity, more through unfocussed material than poor performance. If being mathematical helps, I guess about one fifth is pretty bland stuff, though the multitudes inevitably disagree.

On the other hand, the remainder ranges from the simply enjoyable to the totally masterful.

Supertramp are one of the most *formulated* bands in existence, and I don't mean that in any derogatory sense. It's just that they've worked out a method of achieving intense effect, and they repeat that method through different instumental permutations.

The formula is thus: quiet slow-build acoustic or vocal passage building into electric power crescendo, equals transfixion.

A prime example is the finest song of the set, 'Crime Of The Century', which serves as an encore (led into by 'Two Of Us' from 'Crisis').

Richard Davies, his nasal so-melodic vocal lines wistfully droning behind that simple keyboard backdrip suddenly swings into a cracked scream — "Well roll up and SEE how they've RAPED the UNIVERSE . . ." — dissecting waves of thundering synthesizer. It never works better than on 'Crime', but the technique is applied continually and intelligently as a common factor through the

material, light and apocalyptic shade.

The band remain low key throughout the concert, with the exception of John who dryly chats to the audience between numbers. The rest of the band look fierce, or at least in pain during and after each song. ("If Rick or Roger smile out there then it's really *happening* confides John later).

The visuals are taken care of by (for the most part) simple lighting effects and (towards the close of the set) films.

The band use two short film supplements, one for the last number of the set proper 'Fool's Overture' and one for 'Crime Of The Century'. The former is a short high speed collage, flashing almost imperceptible images of Winston Churchill, the Houses of Parliament, a face under G-strain, and scores more, atmospheric stills all apparently unconnected but striking enough. The latter is a movie representation of the 'Crime' cover, with space-travelling camera leading into trademark disembodies hands clutched to the nether dimension prison bars. Oblique, intense.

The material is taken from the last three albums which, though totally understandable, I find a bit disappointing since I have a curiously unshakable affection for the very first Supertramp album which is probably one of the great lost classics of our time. Still it's obviously a very different band and atmosphere now (though, strangely with 'Even In The Quietest Moments' being self-produced it sounds closer to that far-off debut album than any other in the roster).

The bulk of the material, unsurprisingly, came from the new album and included 'Give A Little Bit', 'Love Boy', (From Now On), 'Even In The Quietest Moments', 'Babaji' and the album's climax 'Fool's Overture'.

And Roger and Rick keep those mouths one

hundred and eighty degrees horizontal, as the sell out house clamour and whistle and bubble and beg for more.

They want a firework display maybe?

ND ON the third day there were interviews. Sort of.

Basically, it's not a pursuit the band enjoy. Bass player Duggie says he doesn't want to do a face-to-face across the table job, which is fair enough, since they usually stink anyway. Instead, he invites us to join him in going to pick up his travelling caravan.

It transpires on the journey that Dougie, along with Roger are the only two who shun travelling between gigs by plane. They take turns at the wheel negotiating huge journeys across America when they could get there much easier and quicker with the rest of the entourage.

"We wanted to see a bit of the place" says Dougie, staring glazed through the wide vista of the mini bus windscreen, "and it's the only way to do it. All the flying messes up your body."

The bus which formerly belonged to Chicago, is comfortable looking and spacious, but long tiring drives are still no joke. Dougie, though, has firm ideas of how to treat himself on tour.

"I've been trying to avoid the junk foods out here, y'know". His Glasgow clipped drawl is undiminished by his time in the States. "It's all rubbish what they eat out here. "Some of us were thinking of getting together in the future to grow our own stuff, become self sufficient. That obviously won't be for a long time though. We've got so many commitments.

"I just hope no-one in Britain has forgotten us. We haven't deserted blighty, we haven't settled anywhere yet. We may even return permanently, eventually."

Most of the Supertramp plans at this moment are vague. They're recording gigs on the current tour with a live album in mind, but it's by no means certain. They have mixed feelings about America (*Crazy* place). They progress through the gruelling tour in an organised plod. When we arrive back at the hotel, it's lunchtime and John comes down to join us. Dougie is reluctant to drink anything but mild ("Ah had an Indian meal last night — a real gut rotter") and does no more than laconically survey the exotic menu.

He grins, pausing over the sweets section. "A nutty tart, eh? I've had a few of those".

Throughout the meal, Dougie more or less falls into silence and John does the talking. He is dour and witty, but recalcitrant when the subject of music is broached. He ventures that he didn't think the sound was very good last night. The only thing he gets interested in is whether the home country thinks the band have deserted them.

"We get worried becuase we're not there and we want to be there. We're worried as to how people feel, thinking that Supertramp have deserted them, the people who made them successful.

"But we haven't necessarily. It's just that there are more people in the world than in England. And anybody who thinks we're tax exiles would see the running costs for this tour. In Britain you just run out of places to play."

Inevitably the subject is raised of whether the band will find the atmosphere very different in Britain now, bearing in mind the radical upsurge its undergone over the past eighteen months. That upsurge is something John is more or less uninformed on, a fact borne out by his supposition that huge dancers bounce about perched on the top of sprung sticks.

John grimaces over his fruit tart but seems unworried to the point of indifference.

"We just do what we do. We don't try and be trendy, we can't alter that. If we become hackneyed and pause then . . ."

His voice trails off, submerged by a mouthful of rhubarb and pastry.

advising men on how to attract women. Most of the songs for the whole album were written during a sound check for a show the band were doing in Copenhagen at Tivoli Gardens. Davies and Hodgson worked the song parts out whilst they sat at a drum kit and Oberheim string synthesiser respectively. It's interesting that writing material in a short space of time seemed to flow better for the band in the case of *Even In The Quietest Moments…* compared to their experiences with writing for the *Crisis? What Crisis?* album. The unpredictable nature of when creativity flows verses the perils of writers block I suppose.

Also, perhaps the pressure on the band to replicate the success they had had with *Crime Of The Century* was maybe less intense than what it was straight after they made that album. Well, whatever the reason was, the creativity just seemed to work when it came to Supertramp writing *Even In The Quietest Moments…* The song 'Fool's Overture' had the working title of 'The String Machine Epic'. It came about as a result of some melodies that Roger had been playing around with on a synthesiser that the band used on stage.

Even In The Quietest Moments… was reviewed by Geoff Barton in *Sounds* under the title, "Give A Little Bit More" in April 1977; "Lazy acoustic guitar playing — strum, strum, strum, it goes, rather nicely. And then a voice drifts in, crooning, 'Ooooh yeah. Alright. Here we go again', and the guitar gets strummed some more. Soon enough, up creep the lyrics, 'Give a little bit, give a little bit of your love to me. Give a little bit, give a little bit of my love to you', and so on, numerous variations of this simple, Framptonesque (sic) theme. Slowly, subtly, the song gathers impetus. A sax parps. A bass thuds neatly into the scheme of things. Vocals, at once slight and solitary, are double tracked, given a little more weight. And the guitar keeps on strumming. After just over four minutes, the song comes to an end. Concise, precisely executed, but on the surface of it no great shakes — totally harmless, completely innocuous in fact. So how come I reckon it's the most stunning song Supertramp have ever put down on vinyl? Hard to say really. While 'Give A Little Bit' — for that is its title — is serene, peaceful, romantic even, I'd say it pulled at my heartstrings but I'm afraid of being branded a sentimentalist, it's as basic as basic can be. Simply beautiful could be the phrase. And I only wish I could find the rest of *Even In The Quietest Moments…* as captivating as this, its opening track. But sadly, after the towering high of the first cut, matters go slowly but steadily downhill. If I can remember correctly, in my largely favourable review of Supertramp's last LP, *Crisis? What Crisis?*, I pondered on the possibility of the band becoming rather too formularised in the future. And in many ways, with this newest, long awaited platter, this possibility has cemented itself into cold hard fact. The remaining three numbers on side one, 'Lover Boy', 'Even In The Quietest Moments…' and 'Downstream' do little more than tread over old ground, could be interchanged with any number on *Crisis? What Crisis?* and you really wouldn't notice the difference. The title track in particular, with its staccato, repetitive chorus-chant of 'Don't you let the sun disappear' brings back recollections of 'Lady'. Side two is better. 'Babaji' and 'From Now On' continue along less than enthralling lines, and the closing number, 'Fool's Overture', brings events down still further. A pity because with this one, a much touted (in the biography at least) 'twelve minute tour-de-force', the band really do try desperately hard to break out of their soft, sensitive musical shell and go off on a new tangent. Unfortunately, it doesn't work out. 'Fool's Overture' is not nearly awesome or dramatic enough to be truly tagged with the label 'magnum opus'. Ostensibly a tale about Britain's sorry economical state ('the island's sinking, let's take to the sky'), we hear Big Ben chiming, Churchill burbling on about something or other, wind whistling and rain falling, together with numerous other sound effects, all running rather clumsily against a song of very little menace or foreboding at all. Maybe 'Fool's Overture' will come alive in the context of a Supertramp concert. We'll have to wait until August at the earliest to see. On the plus side are the band's lyrics, sincere, wholesome but never cringe-inducing and the musicianship of Messrs. Hodgson, Davies, Thomson, Helliwell and Benberg, sheer perfection, never overstated also 'Give A Little Bit' itself. But one hot track out of seven simply isn't good enough, is it?" Reviews are so flipping subjective aren't they? All I can really say in response to this one is that the whole album is worth a listen.

The tour for *Even In The Quietest Moments…* started in Canada. There was much optimism about the live shows. As Hodgson was quoted in April 1977 in *Sounds*; "The set is going to be really amazing. For a start it will be much stronger because we've got three albums to pull material from. We can pick the ones we enjoy playing and the ones which are most popular. It'll be great to play England again. We don't want to lose our English identity. I dread the thought of anyone ever thinking we were an American band. After the American tour we do England, then Europe, some recording, then another American tour, a bit more recording after that, then Japan, Australia, and if we last that long we'll be happy."

Helliwell was quoted in *Record Mirror* in April 1977 as he described the content of the live shows at the time; "We're doing material from *Crime Of The Century* to the new album, using a bit of film — not too much, we don't want to overdo it — a sunrise, montage and a few quick flashes in 'Fool's Overture'." The tour and the album did well. As was reported in *Cash Box* in May 1977, "Supertramp celebrated their recent headlining date at the Los Angeles Forum over dinner and drinks with label executives."

In July 1977 *Cash Box* reported, "After two sold out concerts at Maple Leaf Gardens in Toronto, Supertramp was presented with platinum records for *Even In The Quietest Moments…*". In December 1977, *Cash Box* reported on a presentation to Supertramp in Rotterdam; "Following their recent concert tour of Holland, Supertramp received double gold records for their current LP, *Even In The Quietest Moments…*"

Supertramp were very much in demand in Canada by the time of the *Even In The Quietest Moments…* album. *Billboard* featured an article on the band titled, "Supertramp Nears Status As Top Concert Rock Act" in May 1977; "With its A&M album, *Even In The Quietest Moments…* getting increased airplay on North American FM stations, Supertramp is going after a record in this country as the top concert gross rock act. In its

Pic by Elisabeth Photo Library

SUPERTRAMP: too intimate to operate effectively in the Empire Pool

Pic by Robert Ellis

SUPERTRAMP: 13-date tour in the autumn.

Even in the darkest moments

Supertramp
Empire Pool

INTRIGUING LITTLE combo, Supertramp. I think I may toddle along and see what they're like live.

"Bring a review back with you."

These days you can't even go along to a gig for a bit of piece and quiet without being nabbed for a review (*Stop being tetchy and get on with it, Fielder — Review Ed.*). I don't object normally but when you're sitting among 14,999 people who all know more about Supertramp than you do you kind feel kind of unqualified at times. Particularly when the band is sort of legendary, know what I mean?

But before we even get to the main attraction there's a minor diversion, namely the All-Wembley Paper Aeroplane Throwing Contest which is sponsored by the Blackout-At-The-Flick-Of-A-Switch people. Under the dim emergency lighting attempts are made to entertain us including Mr

Helliwell's tootling solo to 'Hey Jude' but nothing beats the Paper Dart Contest.

Supertramp finally make it on stage at 10.30 after being within a whisker of cancelling the gig but they seem determined to make up to the audience for the delay which is of course entirely beyond their control. They whizzed through their set at a fair rate of knots, scarcely giving the applause a chance to die down before they were off on the next piece.

I found myself being tossed back and forth in much the same way that happens when I listen to their albums although in a curiously different way. Their last three albums evoked widely varying reactions, 'Crisis What Crisis' being the one that affords most satisfaction.

Live, however, the material from 'Even In The Quietest Moments' seems to have much more strength. 'Give A Little Bit', which came fairly early on in the set, marked the point when the sound balance sorted itself out in the band's favour.

Like 'Dreamer' which followed later, 'Give A Little Bit' is one of those genial, tight compositions that simply can't fail. It's A-level pop if you like and the band wisely didn't try to embellish either of them further; they just delivered them in the spirit they were intended.

They are also ideal wedges for longer, more complex pieces like 'Lady' or 'Babaji' which, apart from the obvious favourites, were the best received offerings of the evening. 'Babaji' especially worked excellently, the vocals holding the song together, and the gentle piano refrain at the end achieving an unexpectedly hypnotic character.

But all in all, I did find myself wishing I could be enjoying them in slightly more congenial surroundings. Supertramp's music is too intimate to operate effectively in a chasm like the Empire Pool, particularly Helliwell's woodwind contributions. They lack the grandiose qualities of bands like Genesis or Pink Floyd who can create the awe-inspiring atmosphere that's needed to dominate stadium-sized venues.

They did their best with a fine light show and I know it's difficult when you can sell out the Empire Pool twice over but I felt they might have served themselves better if they'd played an extended run at the Hammersmith Odeon. — **HUGH FIELDER**.

Supertramp back on home tour

SUPERTRAMP return to Britain in October for their first tour for nearly two years. The band, who have based themselves in North America while undertaking a world tour and recording their recently released album, 'Even In The Quietest Moments', have lined up 12 British dates as part of an extensive European tour.

The British dates begin at Birmingham Odeon on October 15 and 16 and continue at Liverpool Empire 17, Manchester Belle Vue 19, Coventry Theatre 21, Newcastle City Hall 24, Glasgow Apollo 26-27, Leicester De Montfort Hall 30, London Wembley Empire Pool November 1-2, Brighton Conference Centre 4, Bournemouth Winter Gardens 7. The tour is being promoted by Peter Bowyer.

Tickets for all gigs except Wembley are priced from £3 downwards and are now on sale by personal application. Wembley tickets — price £3.50 and £2.75 — are now available by postal application from Wembley Empire Pool Box Office (Supertramp), Wembley, HA9, 0DW. Cheques and postal orders should be made payable to 'Wembley Empire Pool (Supertramp)'. Personal applications will be taken from September 2.

A single from the band's latest album, called 'Give A Little Bit', has been released by A&M and is climbing the singles charts.

initial six western Canada concert dates for promoter David Horodezky through Regina, Saskatoon, Winnipeg (two dates at the Arena), Lethbridge, Edmonton and Calgary, the band grossed close to 350,000 dollars. And the band still has to play such major markets as Vancouver, Toronto and Montreal, as well as a number of other smaller cities. An unprecedented two nights at Toronto's Maple Leaf Gardens and the Montreal Forum are in the planning stages for the end of June with the distinct possibility of even a third night in Montreal. In the west there was a slight complication when Roger Hodgson, one of the band's lead vocalists, came down with a cold prior to the Edmonton date before a crowd of 12,000 at the Coliseum. The show went on as planned but in the early part of the concert, Hodgson's voice gave out and the band were forced to change its standard show in order to utilise only material sung by the band's founding member Rick Davies. In a surprise move, the band announced on the stage that it would give a free show at a later

THEY'RE BACK!

PETER BOWYER IN ASSOCIATION WITH ANDREW MILLER PRESENTS

Supertramp

BIRMINGHAM ODEON Saturday 15th October
BIRMINGHAM ODEON Sunday 16th October
LIVERPOOL EMPIRE Monday 17th October
MANCHESTER BELLE VUE Wednesday 19th October
MANCHESTER BELLE VUE Thursday 20th October
COVENTRY THEATRE Friday 21st October
NEWCASTLE CITY HALL Monday 24th October
EDINBURGH USHER HALL Tuesday 25th October
GLASGOW APOLLO Wednesday 26th October
GLASGOW APOLLO Thursday 27th October
LEICESTER DE MONTFORT HALL Sunday 30th October
LONDON EMPIRE POOL Tuesday 1st November
LONDON EMPIRE POOL Wednesday 2nd November
BRIGHTON CONFERENCE CENTRE Friday 4th November
BOURNEMOUTH WINTER GARDEN Monday 7th November
DUBLIN STADIUM Thursday 10th November
DUBLIN STADIUM Friday 11th November
DUBLIN STADIUM Saturday 12th November

WITH SPECIAL GUEST CHRIS DE BURGH

date in Edmonton for those in that night's audience. The crowd was asked to keep ticket stubs and come back to see the show 'as it was supposed to be performed', the following night's concert at the Corral in Calgary was cancelled and it was later announced that the Edmonton and Calgary dates would be rescheduled for the middle of July. It is estimated that it will cost the band close to 40,000 dollars to return to Edmonton to perform a free concert. After the cancellations, Hodgson and Davies, who had also come down with the same virus, and band manager Dave Margereson stayed in Edmonton for a day to get medical advice on the epidemic while the crew and the rest of the band flew on to Calgary. In Canada, Supertramp has taken on supergroup status. Sales of its two albums, *Crime Of The Century* and *Crisis? What Crisis?* have reached double platinum status. Their new LP, *Even In The Quietest Moments…*, debuted on the *Billboard* LP chart at ninety seven with a star in the US."

There exists a rumour that the sheet music placed on the piano on the front cover of the album, whilst titled 'Fool's Overture', is actually 'The Star-Spangled Banner'. It seems that even before their next album, *Breakfast In America*, the band perhaps had a thing or two to say about the place. Who knows precisely what, but still. Besides, I'm stating this information as a rumour because honestly, I don't know but I figure it was worth putting it out there (at least cautiously!) for consideration. Even Supertramp's loyal fan base in Canada was perhaps a bit on the fence about *Even In The Quietest Moments…* . *Record Mirror* reported in June 1977 that the Canadian press reviews "blow hot and cold. Many regard it as great, while just as many say (as happened in the UK), that they could never better *Crime Of The Century*." Oh ye of little faith! Because of course, as history has it, the best was yet to come.

Not long after the release of *Even In The Quietest Moments…* the seed of an idea had perhaps already been planted that the next album needed to be more jovial and less intense. As Roger was quoted in *New Musical Express* in August 1977, "Maybe our choice of songs has been too inclined in one direction. We go for the drama and meaning type things, rather than just breaking out and having a good time for a bit. Perhaps we'll just turn our backs on these three albums (*Crime Of The Century*, *Crisis? What Crisis?* and *Even In The Quietest Moments…*) and make a fun one. But I think everybody feels we'll lose the fans if we do. There's a real strong feeling we should break out on the next album. I think we might do that."

Cash Box reported in September 1978, "During the annual A&M convention, Jerry Moss, Chairman of A&M presented LA based English band Supertramp with a special gold disc for the sales of *Crime Of The Century* LP in France, Germany, Holland and Portugal and for sales of *Even In The Quietest Moments…* in France, Germany and Norway. Supertramp is presently in LA recording a new album entitled *Breakfast In America*."

Chapter Seven:
Breakfast In America (1979)

Breakfast In America (1979)

Rick Davies – keyboards, lead and backing vocals
Roger Hodgson – guitars, keyboards, lead and backing vocals
John Helliwell – saxophones, clarinets, whistles, backing vocals
Dougie Thomson – bass
Bob C. Benberg – drums

Slyde Hyde – tuba and trombone
Gary Mielke – Oberheim programming

Side one
1. Gone Hollywood
2. The Logical Song
3. Goodbye Stranger
4. Breakfast In America
5. Oh Darling

Side two
6. Take The Long Way Home
7. Lord Is It Mine
8. Just Another Nervous Wreck
9. Casual Conversations
10. Child Of Vision

*B*reakfast In America was huge, absolutely huge! Large breakfast fry-up with all the trimmings huge. Supertramp's sixth album was recorded at The Village Recorder in Los Angeles in 1978 and was released on A&M Records in 1979. It gave the band so many successes including the singles in America doing very strongly; 'The Logical Song' got to number six. 'Goodbye Stranger' got to number fifteen. It was reviewed in *Cash Box* in July 1979; "This follow-up to their last top five single, 'The Logical Song', features the intriguing and well paced vocals of Rick Davies and the high back up singing of co-writer Roger Hodgson. Blithe, spirited instrumentation, underscores the lyrical theme of the song. The 'radio only' version of the cut clocks in at four minutes and twenty-five seconds. Hitbound." 'Take The Long Way Home' got to number ten. It was reviewed in October 1979 in *Cash Box*; "The third single off of Supertramp's current top charting LP, which continues to see hot rack and retail action, is a bouncy, up-tempo number laden with pop-symphonic instruments, high pitched vocals and harmonies and a jaunty harmonica figure. This snappy song will no doubt see a good deal of top forty play."

In the UK, the album's title track and 'The Logical Song' were both in the top ten in the singles chart. The album itself won two Grammy Awards in 1980, one for Best Recording Package and the other for Best Engineered Album (non classical category). Other nominations that year included albums from Led Zeppelin and Talking Heads. *Breakfast In America* sold more than four million copies in the US alone and also went to number one in Canada, France, Australia, Norway, Austria and Spain. In 1979, 'The Logical Song' won the Ivor Novello Award for Best Song Musically and Lyrically. By the 1990s, *Breakfast In America* had sold more than eighteen million copies globally and by 2010, that figure had risen to well over twenty million. So many accolades, both big and small! In the 1994 edition of *The Guinness All Time Top 1000 Albums*, *Breakfast in America* was voted in at number two hundred and seven in the all-time greatest rock and pop albums. *Cash Box* reviewed *Breakfast In America* in March 1979; "With its first album in two years, Supertramp has returned with an exquisitely textured, infectiously arranged collection of ten songs composed by group leaders Roger Hodgson and Rick Davies. Throughout the band's career, Supertramp has been noted for its intriguing, sophisticated compositions and gifted ensemble playing, but equally important to *Breakfast In America*'s excellence is the quintet's gift for writing whimsical lyrical statements and engaging narrative accounts. For top forty and AOR formats, A&M is shipping this LP platinum."

'The Logical Song' was reviewed in the singles section in *Cash Box* in March 1979; "Keyboard chording, maracas and imploring singing open this song from Supertramp's new album, *Breakfast In America*. A skilful and probing lyric and a raucous sax line are joined by a familiar circling guitar lick and excellent singing. An emphatic beat adds excitement. Top forty material." In both cases, those reviews turned out to be very prophetic (and then some!).

The band's profile stepped up a gear significantly due to the *Breakfast In America* album. As was advocated in *Billboard* in March 1979; "This sophisticated English quintet graduated from a cult to a mass group since its last album, *Even In The Quietest Moments…*, nearly two years ago. Its newest work again is centred around the layered keyboard wizardry of writers Rick Davies and Rodger Hodgson and the woodwinds of John Helliwell. While the group rocks out, it is best on its introspective ballads and mid-tempo fare with poetic lyrics and lushly arranged orchestrations. The album's catchiest and most incisive track is 'The Logical Song' that is ably augmented by other songs that dig deep into the human situation. Amazingly, the group produces a full sound without a lead guitarist. Bassist Dougie Thomson and drummer Bob Benberg round out the group."

Bedsit blunderings

Supertramp
Wembley Arena

FIVE AGEING hippies occupied the stage of Wembley Arena on Wednesday night to deliver a lengthy concert dedicated to pre-punk pomp and circumstance.

Sentimental, world weary and purveyors of homespun philosophies, Supertramp in British rock terms are virtually an anachronism. Yet they still filled Wembley Arena for four nights and their album 'Breakfast In America' has shifted nine million copies to date.

Doubtless this band have got used to the critical blows aimed at them by the rock press and redman John Helliwell repeated to the audience a certain London evening rag's condemnation that their act was too 'cosy' with the self-satisfied air of a man

who has smirked all the way to the bank more than once. Giving the people what they want is an easy option that Supertramp are gonna have to increasingly fall back on if they continue to peddle the vapid material that has always been their hallmark.

Each number was generally over long, ponderous and lethargic, no energy, no drive, no commitment. A collection of notes welded together like pieces of Meccano — classical piano intro, overlaid with inoffensive guitar, pointless sax and forgettable drums. Excitement never got a look in. 'Dreamer', a song that ought to be played with paranoid intensity, was blunderingly introduced as a 'rock' number and performed in such a weak manner as to render it worthless.

Lyrically Supertramp were the pits, the kind of stuff a ten year old would write and

immediately throw in the nearest dustbin. How can grown men keep a straight face when singing a love song with lines like 'You were the reason I was born' – probably the most hackneyed cliche in the whole of romantic writing. Other examples were endless; this bunch constantly wallowed in the self pity that bedsit troubadours like Al Stewart used to make a whole industry out of.

The audience, of course, lapped it all up especially when told that the concerts were being taped for a live album. To me, it was simply depressing. If there are any of you out there who laugh at the punk assertion that the performers are simply an extension of the punters, Supertramp showed how condescending rock artists can be and that sometimes the gulf between stage and audience is as wide as the Grand Canyon.

CHRIS RYAN

SUPERTRAMP'S Richard Davies enjoys a good laugh

Pic: Gus Stewart

A regular slog

SUPERTRAMP
'Breakfast In America'
A&M (AMLK 63708)* ½**

IF SUPERTRAMP have any clearly identifiable public image at all, it is probably closest to that of, say, Pink Floyd — introspective elitists too bound up in evolving their own 'art' to bother with we mere mortals, faceless perfectionists more concerned with creating still more intricate masterworks than taking any notice of how young Norman Normal gets his musical kicks. New Wave, what's that? Some kind of hairstyle?

Moving house to the luxurious climes of Los Angeles (the Sodom and Gomorrah of rock 'n' roll) and giving the kind of ultra-bland interview that they did with the whispering teeth on the Whistle Test t'other week have only helped reinforce that BOF brand stamped on their collective foreheads.

The truth, however, is that, while Supertramp may not give the world's most rivetting interviews (so not everyone's got a mouth like Ted Nugent) and while they may be more than a little fastidious when it comes to their music (this album took nearly a year in the making), they've conquered and cultivated their own particular corner of the musical sphere. Their elaborately structured, largely keyboard dominated style may not be to everyone's taste, but blind prejudice cannot conceal Supertramp's prowess as musicians or the quality of this album.

Perhaps my strongest criticism of 'Breakfast In America' is that, while it's vintage Supertramp, it's also rather stereotyped Supertramp; establishing an individual and recognisable style is important, but so is developing and furthering that style, and 'Breakfast' hardly represents Supertramp striding manfully in some brave new direction.

On the positive side, 'Breakfast' has some memorable songs, occasionally inspired musicianship and a production gloss that fair glistens in the dark. The collective pens of joint vocalists Rick Davies and Roger Hodgeson have lost none of their sharpness, the most impressive examples being 'The Logical Song' (which would make the ideal single with its catchy simplicity), 'Goodbye Stranger' (a slowly building track driven along by the subtly understated drumming of Bob C Benberg), the rather more grandiose 'Just Another Nervous Wreck' and the title track itself, a quirkly constructed vision of the States with a slow, thudding march-along beat and jazz-tinged reed embellishments from John Helliwell. Indeed, for me, Helliwell is the star of the show with his consistently inventive saxophone breaks lifting the album out of its occasional moments of insipidness.

DAVID LEWIS

Under the title, "Supertramp's Platinum Breakfast", *Cash Box* reported in June 1979; "Supertramp were recently awarded a platinum album for their current release, *Breakfast In America*. The presentation was made at the Market Diner, where the party was held after Supertramp's performance at Madison Square Garden."

Similarly in the April of that year, *Record World* reported on how Supertramp were honoured at a party attended by A&M executives in LA's Forum Club following their concert at the Forum. There was certainly a lot of success to be celebrated at the time and as such, many celebrations took place. It sounds like the live shows were quite the party too. As was reported in *Record World* in May 1979 of a live show in Nashville; "Supertramp played a solid two and a half hour set to a small but eager crowd at Municipal Auditorium here 9th May. The show featured many musical and sound delights, along with a spectacular light show and other visual treats throughout the evening. Musically the concert featured a little something for everyone, from intense modern electric rock to ballads to mood pieces to jazz. High musicianship and enthusiasm by Supertramp dominated the show. Audience reaction was highest to the material from the *Breakfast In America* LP, which included 'Take The Long Way Home', 'The Logical Song' and 'Child Of Vision' as well as earlier works like 'Give A Little Bit'. The group nearly stole their own show with the special lighting effects and theatrical stage set… These visuals and lighting effects, produced in-house by Supertramp's Enlightening Lights, were topped only by the Delicate Acoustics in-house sound. In this acoustically muddy hall, vocals and instruments all came out clearly as the entire audio effect. Other treats not to be believed included a segment with a dancing banana and coffee shop waitress during 'Breakfast In America'."

As with the *Even In The Quietest Moments…* album, Rick and Roger wrote material for *Breakfast In America* separately. Although the concept for the album was conceived between them both in person, the song writing process was not predominantly collaborative. Ironically perhaps, the duo's original idea for an album theme was going to be something about their conflict of ideals. Fortunately, the idea was terminated in favour of doing something more fun and that's how *Breakfast In America* came about. Some listeners considered *Breakfast In America* to be a satirical comment on American society and culture but the band insisted that this was not the case and that any such misconception is purely coincidental — in the same way that people thought *Crime Of The Century* was a concept album when the band stipulated that it wasn't.

Breakfast In America was reviewed in *Rolling Stone* in June 1979; "*Breakfast In America* is a textbook-perfect album of post-Beatles, keyboard-centered English art rock that strikes the shrewdest possible balance between quasi-symphonic classicism and rock and roll. Whereas Supertramp's earlier LPs were bogged down by swatches of meandering, Genesis-like esoterica, the songs here are extraordinarily melodic and concisely structured, reflecting these musicians' saturation in American pop since their move to Los Angeles in 1977. Supertramp's major problem is an increasing dichotomy between their rhapsodic aural style and a glib, end-of-the-empire pessimism. The music in 'Gone Hollywood' is so suffused with romantic excitement that it's difficult to believe the ennui the lyrics claim: 'So many creeps in Hollywood/…Ain't nothin' new in my life today'. Though laced with nice, Beach Boys-style falsettos, 'Goodbye Stranger', an uncharacteristically happy fantasy about endless one-night stands, seems far more honest. But the only cut that really wrestles the dichotomy is 'The Logical Song'. In this small masterpiece, singer Roger Hodgson enacts an Everyman who excoriates an education that preaches categorical jargon instead of knowledge and sensitivity. 'And they showed me a world where I could be so dependable, clinical, intellectual, cynical', he declaims, reeling off three and four syllable assonances with a schoolboy's tongue in cheek worthy of Ray Davies and the Kinks. Flamenco flourishes and a hot sax break help deflate the tune's self-pity with a wonderfully wry humor. The next 'logical' thing for these guys to do with their awesome technique is to turn it more toward this sort of ironic drollery. Then Supertramp might become not only the best-sounding art-rock band in existence, but one of the most interesting."

An interesting review indeed. Admittedly, my interpretation of it is that it appears that the reviewer is really trying to delve into the meaning of some of the lyrics there, perhaps more so than Supertramp themselves intended! One of the fascinating things about Supertramp's music and the *Breakfast In America* album in particular is that there are so many infinite possibilities as to what the lyrics of each song could actually mean.

In some interviews, insights into the meanings behind some songs have been offered by the band but even then, there is often a lot of metaphor and scope for interpretation there. For instance, in an interview with *Rolling Stone* in February 2012, the interviewer asked Roger Hodgson if 'Take The Long Way Home' was about a disconnect between being on stage and his family life, to which Hodgson clarified when he was quoted, "Unlike most of my songs, that one wasn't autobiographical. That one was kind of a two-level song. And when I said it's hard going home to the wife because she treats you like part of the furniture, that wasn't my reality then anyway. I actually wrote it just as I was getting together with my future wife, so family hadn't really hit me then — it came later, it became truer. But it was kind of a play on words that suddenly took on a depth, too, about reaching later in life and having regrets that you didn't do what you wanted to do."

Also regarding 'Take The Long Way Home', Hodgson was quoted in February 2012 in *Classic Rock Revisited*; "It wasn't consciously about people I knew. There is a double meaning to that song. There is the obvious meaning of taking the long way home when you don't want to get back home to your wife but there is a deeper meaning of taking the long way home about what really has meaning in life. You can take the long way home to your heart. You can look back on your life and wonder where it has gone. You wonder where the meaning of life has disappeared to. It is an interesting song on two levels. The last chorus talks about looking at your life and wondering what you could have been if you'd had more time. It has the lightweight meaning of your wife treating you like a piece of the furniture and then you get thrown a heavy line about where your life has gone. It has an interesting duality."

The same month In *Rolling Stone*, Hodgson was quoted as he discussed what 'The Logical Song' meant to him; "I had a lot of questions going on. I don't know if I can say it was wisdom, it was more the songs were true to who I was back then and I think that was why they kind of stand up. Maybe I've learned a bit more now and I'm a bit older and wiser, but the songs still feel very relevant, most of them. And that's pretty amazing, considering how young I was at the time."

Also regarding 'The Logical Song', Hodgson was quoted in *Classic Rock Revisited* in February 2012; "I don't know if I was in tune with human nature, I just had those questions going on in me and I wanted to express them. Early adulthood can be a very confusing time. You learn all of these things in school and then you are thrown out into the world and you're expected to have all of the answers. I didn't have any of the answers. I certainly hadn't found the answers to the deeper questions in school. The song was very autobiographical. I knew how to be sensible, logical and cynical but I didn't have a clue who I was. To me, that is the life journey we are on; to find out who we are and what life is. They don't teach you that in school. I get a lot of emails from younger people today and they tell me that song totally captures what is going on with their lives."

Hodgson elaborated on 'The Logical Song' in *Rolling Stone* the same month in terms of how it struck a chord with people, even in 1979 when disco music was overridingly predominant in the charts at the time; "It's a good song. I/we never really paid attention to what was happening in the world of music. I know different fashions came and went, but we just did our own thing and the critics and media didn't really know what to do with us, some liked us, most kind of discarded us because we weren't what was in vogue. But yeah, there was a huge disco thing happening when *Breakfast In America* came out and yet somehow we broke through it and found a place on radio. And the great thing is these songs are still played today, which is pretty amazing."

Supertramp's show at Wembley Arena was reviewed in *Sounds* in November 1979; "Five ageing hippies occupied the stage of Wembley Arena on Wednesday night to deliver a large lengthy concert dedicated to pre-punk pomp and circumstance. Sentimental, world weary and purveyors of homespun philosophies, Supertramp in British rock terms are virtually an anachronism. Yet they still filled Wembley Arena for four nights and their album, *Breakfast In America*, has shifted nine million copies to date. Doubtless this band have got used to the critical blows aimed at them by the rock press and reedman John Helliwell repeated to the audience at a certain London evening rag's condemnation that their act was too 'cosy' with the self satisfied air of a man who has smirked all the way to the bank more than once. Giving the people what they want is an easy option that Supertramp are gonna have to increasingly fall back on if they continue to peddle the vapid material that has always been their hallmark. Each number was generally over long, ponderous and lethargic, no energy, no drive, no commitment. A collection of notes welded together like pieces of Meccano — classical piano intro, overlaid with inoffensive guitar, pointless sax and forgettable drums. Excitement never got a look in. 'Dreamer', a song that ought to be played with paranoid intensity, was blunderingly introduced as a 'rock' number and performed in such a weak manner as to render it worthless. Lyrically, Supertramp were the pits, the kind of stuff a ten year old would write and immediately throw in the nearest dustbin. How can grown men keep a straight face when singing a love song with lines like 'You were the reason I was born' — probably the most hackneyed cliché in the whole of romantic writing. Other examples were endless. This bunch constantly wallowed in the self pity that bedsit troubadours Al Stewart used to make a whole industry out of. The audience of course, lapped it all up especially when told that the concerts were being taped for a live album. To me, it was simply depressing. If there are any of you out there who laugh at the punk assertion that the performers are simply an extension of the punters, Supertramp showed how condescending rock artists can be and that sometimes the gulf between stage and audience is as wide as the Grand Canyon."

I don't think I am the only one who, whilst reading the whole review by Chris Ryan, was thinking to myself this reviewer would much rather be at a punk concert and I'm sure he made that decision even before he had passed the ticket bods at Wembley Arena. Lots of bands who did a large body of their work in the seventies seemed to have this challenge at the time of the explosion of punk music as in, they were panned purely for not being in vogue rather than for any other reason. The reviewer seems to have been disparaging of Supertramp throughout his contribution and his attitude is exemplified with good humour as he captioned a photo of Rick Davies looking very serious; "Supertramp's Richard Davies enjoys a good laugh." Supertramp weren't punk and they weren't disco at a time when a lot of groups felt the need to be in order to be successful. I think that really brings home the fact that they achieved something incredible with *Breakfast In America*.

Hodgson was quoted in November 2007 in *Goldmine* as he advocated for the importance of not trying to pander to external influences when creating music; "Supertramp was always out of step with the times, out of step with fashion. And you know, it was our blessing and our curse. I mean, we never looked at the world and thought, 'Oh my God, we've got to do a disco record' or 'we gotta do this because that's what's happening out there'. We were just doing our own thing, and we didn't even have any guidelines within the band, you know. We just sort of enjoyed all of it, and we didn't. The great thing about it was we didn't censor ourselves or limit ourselves, or I didn't anyway, and I think that's the secret. I think when you start doing that — which I've fallen into, I've fallen into that hole when you start trying to come up with a hit, or trying to create an album that's going to fit with the current music scene - you're doomed."

The appeal of 'The Logical Song' is arguably universally relatable. It asks questions that we have probably all had about life at some point or other. Hodgson's talent seems to be so prevalent in how he put such deep philosophical ponderings into such a musically enjoyable song. He was quoted in February 2011 in the *North County Times*; "I've always had a lot of questions, deep questions like 'Why am I here? Where do I find God? How do I find true love?' I started writing songs when I was twelve, and I put my questions and my feelings into my songs. Within a year, I actually did my first concert at school of all original songs. In 'The Logical Song', I'm looking for the answers I didn't get in school. They taught me how to be sensible and intellectual and responsible and all these things. But, at the end of the day I was left with 'please tell me who I am', that to me was the most important question and has been for most of my life."

'Gone Hollywood' is the opening track on *Breakfast In America*. It was written by Rick Davies and tells the story of a person who moves to Los Angeles with hopes of becoming a movie star. The song is about the struggles and frustrations of how within such hopes and dreams, the reality doesn't match. The story in the song has a positive outcome though; the person gets his big break and eventually becomes "the talk of the Boulevard", a much more positive and lighthearted opener than 'School' on the *Crime Of The Century* album. Perhaps the fun and positivity featured on *Breakfast In America* was one of the ingredients that helped enable the album's global success on such a scale. That said, some of the sentiments expressed in 'The Logical Song' aren't strictly a bed of roses.

The album's closing track, 'Child Of Vision', features some beautifully long solo parts with the Wurlitzer piano being used as the main instrument. The track fades out with a short saxophone solo by John Helliwell. In June 1979, Helliwell's approach to the meanings in *Breakfast In America* was quoted in *Melody Maker*; "It's a mistake to read too deeply into the lyrics. Sure, the tone does poke a finger at certain elements of the American lifestyle but no more than that."

In the same interview, Bob Siebenberg was quoted; "I don't think it (*Breakfast In America*) was meant as a big social comment." Hodgson was quoted in the same feature in *Melody Maker* as he described how people looking for meaning in the lyrics of *Breakfast In America* was essentially "a hangover from the days of *Crime Of The Century*" and elaborated that *Breakfast In America* was "just a collection of songs. We chose the title because it was a fun title. It suited the fun feeling of the album. There are a few comments on America but it wasn't premeditated… The songs on the album were chosen because we really wanted to get a feeling of fun and warmth across. I think we felt that we had done three pretty serious albums — *Crime Of The Century, Crisis? What Crisis?* and *Even In The Quietest Moments…* — and it was about time we showed the lighter side of ourselves."

The album went through two rounds of demos due to the fact that both Davies and Hodgson had worked on material separately at home. The first round of demos consisted of Davies and Hodgson playing through their individually written material on the piano with their own vocals. The second round of demos were eight tracks that had been recorded at Southcombe Studios in California during April and May 1978. The demos were used by the band to work out the backing track arrangements for all of the songs apart from 'Take The Long Way Home'.

Producer and engineer for the album, Peter Henderson, was quoted in *Sound On Sound* in July 2005; "I went to LA thinking we were going to start recording, but nothing was quite ready, so we ended up doing very, very basic eight-track demos for the whole album. As it turned out, this was a good opportunity to work out the arrangements for most of the backing tracks — 'Take The Long Way Home' wouldn't arrive until much later in the project — and we even assembled the running order for the album. We were pretty organised. The home demos of each song were pretty much all keyboard-based — vocal and piano or vocal and Wurlitzer — and then (at Southcombe) the whole band would run through them. However, by the time we completed the eight-track demos, we didn't have any of the parts that would be overdubbed on the finished record. We just worked on the live backing tracks and overdubbed the guide vocals."

To avoid having to rearrange the content that was already there, the band and their production team dedicated a week to trying out various sound setups until they found one that worked. Unfortunately though, it emerged to be a wasted effort due to the fact that it was felt that more time was needed to get things just right. It didn't seem to be too much of a problem though; Henderson was quoted in the same article in *Sound On Sound* as he recalled how well Hodgson and Davies seemed to be getting on at the time; "They got along fantastically well and everyone was really happy. There was a very, very good vibe and I think everyone was really buoyed up by the recordings and A&M's response to them." Such things are certainly subjective though and it was not felt by others that all was well.

The iconic cover art on *Breakfast In America* features actress Kate Murtagh dressed as "Libby", the waitress from an American diner. Behind her is a view of New York City through an aeroplane window. "Libby" is holding a small plate in one hand and the glass of orange juice on it replaces the torch on the Statue of Liberty. The album's title is written on the restaurant menu that she is holding in her other hand. The background features Manhattan made of a cornflake box, ashtray, cutlery, egg boxes and condiments all spray painted white. The back cover photo features Supertramp having breakfast whilst reading newspapers from their respective hometowns.

In June 1979, *Record World* advocated that on the basis of Supertramp's success of *Breakfast In America*, "this deliberately low-profiled quintet looks in danger of becoming instantly recognisable." The success of *Breakfast In America* was worth huge amounts of money, especially to A&M who, on the back of such success, as was reported the same feature, "readied an extensive merchandising, advertising, marketing and promotion campaign built around (the album's) cover art and its jocular heroine, Libby."

Breakfast In America scored so much consistency when it came to getting positive reviews. I actually think it would be necessary to search far and wide to find a review that has anything tremendously bad to say about the album or indeed, any of the singles from it. By the time of *Breakfast In America*, Supertramp had certainly come a long way since the days of that harsh review from *Rolling Stone* in January 1976 ("the biggest crisis is trying to get through both sides of this record")! On balance, in July 1979, it was argued in *The Village Voice* that *Breakfast In America* was a "hooky album" that merely evoked "random grunts" of pleasure. Hmmm, whilst the review in *The Village Voice* was certainly not a glowing one, it was equally not one of complete dissatisfaction either.

Upon the release of *Breakfast In America*, Supertramp's live sets still included many songs from their previous albums. Such live set was well reviewed in the *St Louis Post Despatch* in March 1979; "Supertramp performs rock at Checkerdome… There wasn't much in the way of theatrics as Supertramp opened a two day run at Checkerdome on Sunday night. But what there was of it was effective. Moreover, the crowd of 13,700 — a sellout — was treated to an absolutely excellent set. Sell-outs are relative. Almost 20,000 persons can be jammed into the Checkerdome. The British quintet however, did not want the 6,000 seats behind the stage sold. They decided instead to perform two shows. Tonight's performance was not quite a sell-out yet. The band had Roger Hodgson on vocals, keyboards and guitars. Rick Davies on vocals and keyboards, Dougie Thomson on bass, John Helliwell on reeds and Bob C. Benberg on drums. Hodgson, Davies and Helliwell move around from instrument to instrument so often during a single song that they ought to wear numbers. It wasn't visually disturbing but it was difficult to keep track of who was doing what. But whatever, they're doing it right. There are all kinds of categories for rock — from hard to country to jazz. In the case of Supertramp's music, a new category has to be added — delightful. Their music is so well-threaded that what the members of the band were doing was easy to appreciate. The concert opened with 'School' from the *Crime Of The Century* album. Davies played a few notes on the harmonica and then Hodgson sang. It was all rather delicate, even when the others joined in. After a jazz-rock number, they performed two songs from their *Breakfast In America* album, including the title song and an absolutely delightful composition called 'Goodbye Stranger' in which Helliwell, Hodgson and Davies sang falsetto in unison. 'Sister Moonshine' from the *Crisis? What Crisis?* album featured Hodgson on acoustic guitar. There was a short bit in here with Davies on the harmonica and Helliwell on the clarinet that made the song even more interesting. 'Hide In Your Shell' had Hodgson, Helliwell and Davies on keyboards at the same time. They did that again on a couple of occasions. 'From Now On' was pleasant but for me, 'Even In The Quietest Moments…' was one of the highlights of the concert. Hodgson on the acoustic guitar opened and was joined for a time by Helliwell on clarinet, and then it was just Hodgson again. It was really nice. One of their two bits of theatrics occurred at the end of 'Asylum' number where a 'giant banana' came on stage to dance with a 'female ape' dressed in a nurse's uniform. The other was during a playing of 'Rudy' when there was a motion picture of a train moving at high speed through a crowded area. Supertramp accompanied the movie with some fascinating train music. 'Give A Little Bit', one of their hits, had Hodgson back on acoustic guitar and Helliwell on alto sax. 'The Logical Song' had the audience cheering — not an unusual occurrence, but it was done with much more gusto. For 'Dreamer' and 'If Everyone Was Listening' there was so much going on musically that it was difficult to keep track of who was doing what and to which instruments. But whatever they were doing, they did it right. It sounded wonderful."

The success of *Breakfast In America* in the US was such that it rekindled interest in Supertramp's earlier albums. As was reported in *Melody Maker* in June 1979; "The success in the States of *Breakfast In America* — it has spent six weeks at the top of the *Cash Box* chart — has reactivated interest in the band's two formative albums, *Crime Of The Century* and *Even In The Quietest Moments…* which have crept back into the charts. The new Supertramp single, 'Breakfast In America', which has just been released in Britain, clocked up more than 100,000 advance orders in British record shops." Notably, in the same article, it was stipulated that Supertramp were due to book some tour dates in Britain. Evidently, there was much anticipation and excitement about the band coming back from America to their home ground at this time.

Hodgson was quoted in *Classic Rock Revisited* in February 2012 as he described some of his experiences of how audiences have reacted to the varying moods of different songs on the album; "As an artist, and as a human being, I feel incredibly humbled by that. It is a wonderful gift that I'm able to give. For whatever reason, I've not been afraid to share my deepest longing, pain and joy and that is what my songs have related. 'Breakfast In America' is a fun sing-along type of song and then I go to something like 'Lord Is It Mine?' which is a much more deep and emotional, soul searching and questioning song that came from deep in my heart. Because I am able to take people on a range of emotions — they all have relationships with these songs and they touch a nerve. I look out and I see people laughing and I see people crying and I see couples hugging each other and it is a wonderful feeling, as an artist, to be able to give that to people."

John Helliwell was quoted in February 1988 in *Cash Box*; "Originally in the middle to late seventies the audience was a college crowd. With the success of *Breakfast In America* it expanded quite dramatically to young and old. It obviously depends on the current success you have in a particular country."

Roger Hodgson said he had faith in *Breakfast In America* right from the days of making the album. He was quoted in June 1979 in *Melody Maker*; "I always knew it was going to be a huge album, I knew our time had come and if it hadn't happened, the big man in the sky was playing a trick on us. I felt that it had to happen, the mere fact that we had to struggle so long for it."

He was quoted in *Classic Rock Revisited* in February 2012 as he described the mood of optimism among the band whilst making *Breakfast In America*; "I think we all had a sense. There was expectancy and we were poised for this album. We had done a lot of touring and we were primed for it. It was a time where radio was king and with this particular collection of songs we felt that we had the songs that would get on the radio. That is why I fought to really get it right. We all had our different roles. I was really the main producer and the driving force. I was the last one that was to say that it was done. I think everyone else trusted that I knew what I was doing because I had come up with the goods up to that point. We had to keep going until I said that we got it."

Such was Hodgson's belief in the project that he had really given it his all. For the last two months of completing *Breakfast In America*, he had parked a camper van outside the recording studio in order that he could dedicate his time to mixing the album and catching some sleep in brief periods of rest in between. He was quoted as he explained the logistics of the situation in *Classic Rock Revisited* in February 2012; "All albums are hard to complete. That one took eight months to complete. For the last two months I was actually sleeping in the studio. I parked my camper outside the door and at four o'clock in the morning I would collapse in the camper and then at ten o'clock in the morning we would start again. We were trying to get done before the tour started, which was looming in front of us. I was tenacious and I couldn't rest until we got the mixes right. Back in those days, we didn't have computers; we did everything manually. We had to keep at it until we got it right."

In his interview with *Classic Rock Revisited* in February 2012, Roger asserted that the line in the song in 'Breakfast In America' that goes, "What's she got? Not a lot?" was contributed by Rick Davies. The song overall, as with 'Dreamer' on the *Crime Of The Century* album, was written by Roger at his mum's house. He was quoted in the same interview; "I wrote that song in my mum's living room; I was either eighteen or nineteen years old and I had just bought a pump organ. I found one in the English countryside in a church. When the churches went to electric organs they put all of the pump organs in the back room. I scoured the churches for a pump organ. I don't remember why I wanted a pump organ so badly but I finally found one and I bought it for twenty six pounds. I took it home and 'Breakfast In America' was the first thing I wrote on it." Wow!

Imagine 'Breakfast In America' played entirely on a pump organ. I bet that would sound awesome.

March 1979 marked Supertramp's tenth anniversary as a band. *Breakfast In America* signified how far they had come in that decade. From uncertain beginnings to reaching superstar status globally. *Breakfast In America* was the band's sixth album and it was the one that was demonstrative of the success of the song writing partnership between Davies and Hodgson. 1979 was an incredible year for Supertramp as their records dominated turntables around the world and AM and FM radio play. This success was such that the tour was pretty much non stop. The band's live show in the late November part of the tour at the Pavilion in Paris was recorded and released under the name, *Paris*. The logic behind making the *Paris* album was to avoid an excessively long gap between albums. After the intense success and touring of *Breakfast In America*, the band had very reasonably decided that they would need a hiatus. The *Paris* album served the band well and the live version of 'Dreamer' was released as a single where it went to number one in Canada and number fifteen in America. Ironic really, considering that the studio version had failed to chart there in 1974. That said, the aspiration to do a live album had seemingly been there for a while.

Helliwell was quoted in *Record Mirror* in April 1977; "We want to do a live album before we get round to the next studio one, probably by the end of the year. All we've done before are radio concert broadcasts. We got the idea of doing a live album — or albums even — from listening to one of them in Tokyo of all places. The band has an excitement live that we can't get in the studios and it would be great if we were able to capture that."

The hectic nature of life on the road for Supertramp is well documented in an extended feature from *Billboard* in July 1979. It is quite a long piece but I make no apologies for quoting the article in its entirety because it really does get across the ways in which *Breakfast In America* was life changing for the band. The article was appropriately titled, "A Day In The Life Of Supertramp";

"Supertramp is a family on the road. This successful UK group has had a number one LP to inspire fans to attend its cross country concerts. *Billboard*'s Roman Kozak went on the road with the group to see how life is for a top money act. This is his report: Pittsburgh — It is almost 3pm when the five members of Supertramp and their entourage arrive at the Pittsburgh Hyatt House Hotel, which is located across the street from the 13,000 seat Civic Arena where the band will be playing later that evening. The road crew is already there, preparing the stage within the cavernous hall (where there was a Jesus '79 festival the night before) into a venue hosting a state of-the-art rock show. As the band arrives in town its LP, *Breakfast In America*, is entering its fourth week at number one on the LP chart, but this industrial city of about 600,000 people is offering no hero's welcome. Nor is any expected. The Pittsburgh date is the beginning of the last leg of a sixty city tour, which will end with three nights at Alpine Valley near Milwaukee. After that, the band will begin work on a Canadian trek, and then go to Europe. It is not just in the US where Supertramp's brand of melodic and sophisticated English art rock has captivated audiences. The band has also broken through in Britain, Germany, Holland, Scandinavia, Australia and New Zealand. On the day it is playing Pittsburgh, the band's management estimates that it is selling more than 100,000 LPs daily in just the US alone but at the door of the Hyatt House this is difficult to believe. Except for their denim and hair the members of the Supertramp party are as prosaic and businesslike as the Pennsylvania Petroleum Institute members staying at the same hotel. Nobody recognises them."

"Supertramp played in Indianapolis the night before, and all the members had flown to Pittsburgh that morning, which is a slight departure from routine, since wherever possible the individual members of the band travel from gig to gig by rented car. Unlike virtually every rock band that can afford it (and many who can't) Supertramp never travels by limo. The trip from airport to hotel is by taxi. Also unlike in most rock bands, the two principal members travel with their wives. Sue Davies, the American wife of composer/vocalist/keyboard player Rick Davies, is in charge of the merchandising on the tour, while Roger Hodgson, the other songwriter and vocalist/guitarist/keyboard player of the group, usually travels by house trailer along with his wife, Karuna, and their infant, Heidi, who was born in the trailer just before the band played in San Diego April 7."

"With his wispy beard, Indian shirts and sandals, Hodgson is the warmest and most approachable of the group, while at the same time looking the most fragile and ethereal. He says assisting with the birth, and then facing an audience almost immediately afterwards was among the greatest of all experiences in his lifetime. 'The band acts as it does, low key, no big deals, no stars, no limousines, because it has been on the road long enough and has seen enough of the craziness that this is its way of keeping its sanity and sense of normality through these long trips', explains Charly Prevost, the blond and unruffled representative of Mismanagement Inc., Supertramp's management company, who takes care of the band's needs on the road."

The feature continues, "Altogether five tractor trailers full of equipment and thirty three people ('eleven double rooms and eleven singles', counts Prevost) make the trip when Supertramp travels from city to city. Mark Roper is the tour manager, Russell Pope, who is credited on the albums, takes care of the sound, and 'Spy' Matthews is the production manager. Mark Felton, who counts out one hundred dollars in expense money in the hotel lobby for Hodgson — and gets a signed receipt — takes care of the band's finances. The manager of the band, Dave Margereson, stays in Los Angeles, where the English band is now based. Most of the people on the tour have worked together for at least the last three years and know each other well. A major rock tour, with its long hours, endless miles, hurry up and wait schedules, lack of sleep, and various ego problems between a group of people who must stay in constant close physical proximity to each other, breeds its own tensions and conflicts. But with Supertramp, at least in Pittsburgh, there is none of that."

"The good humour and patience that the musicians and crew show not just to an outside journalist, but also to each other during the day and the next morning make for an almost boring assignment. But there is little time for conflict or anything else once the band arrives in town. Two of its members, Hodgson and bass player Dougie Thomson are obliged to leave for a local radio station to tape an interview almost immediately after arriving at the hotel. The others can relax, watch television or explore the neighbourhood before the 6pm sound check. 'Dougie and I usually do the radio interview, while the others do the store things. It may be because the others are not smart enough to do radio', jokes Hodgson on the way to the car belonging to Chuck Gullo, A&M's local marketing man who will drive the group to WDVE-FM where the interview is to be held. Though there is no time for it this trip. Supertramp has built a base of goodwill through the years among the retailing community by visiting local stores and distributors and personally passing out concert tickets to staffers. With Ted Nugent on the radio not exactly pleasing all of the Oldsmobile's six occupants, Gullo, a Cleveland resident, gets lost on the way to the station in nearby downtown Pittsburgh. His wandering takes the crew by the Stanley Theatre, a 3,500 seater owned by DiCesare-Engler who are also promoting the Supertramp concert at the Civic Arena. Located at the edge of downtown Pittsburgh's rather unprepossessing porno district, the art-deco Theatre has been named by *Billboard* as the nation's top venue of its size, according to a sign on the door. Two nights before Supertramp arrived, Journey played there, with Eddie Rabbitt due a week later. While Pittsburgh is hardly a major music centre, music is there for those who want it. It is visited by virtually every attraction that tours the country, so that a major act is playing in town almost every week, either at the Civic Arena, the Stanley, or for R&B and disco groups, the Holiday House in suburban Monroeville. The top live club in town is the Decade, located near the Uni of Pittsburgh campus. In suburban Pittsburgh, the 2001 clubs chain has two clubs, while fashionable downtown discos include the Bank Library, which is in an old bank building and Happy Landing whose 'no denim' sign on the door means it is little interested in the designer jeans crowd."

"WDVE FM, where the two musicians finally arrive at 4pm, a half hour late, is the top FM rock station in town. Upon arrival at the station, Hodsgon and Thomson are ushered into a small room where they will be interviewed by Dennis Benson, producer of *Backstage Special*, a syndicated programme mixing artist interviews with some of their music. No music is actually played during the interview. That will be added later when the tape is edited and Benson's voice is taken out and replaced with that of a disk jockey with a more mellifluous voice. The interview begins with the usual questions about the band's origins and name, with Hodgson more at ease in answering and the wiry and muscular Thomson at first seeming more tense, though he too, soon relaxes. The name of the band, says Hodgson, comes from the 1910 book, *Autobiography of A Supertramp* by R.H. Davis, 'but if we had known what trouble we would have with the name in the US, we may never have picked it', adds Hodgson, 'here they thought we were some sort of English version of the New York Dolls, because tramp means something different in Britain and the US. In Britain it just means a hobo, while here it seems to imply all sorts of things about fallen women or prostitutes.' *Breakfast In America*, the last LP, entered the *Billboard* charts in late March of this year, climbing all the way to number one where it remained for four weeks, before slipping down to two. However, it was displaced by Donna Summer's *Bad Girls* for only one week before popping right back to the top. The musicians have told the story of Supertramp's origins many times before and the answers come easy, but when the two are asked about the source of their creative powers, they have to pause and think for a while, 'I think there is a creative force that runs through everything', ventures Hodgson, 'I try to be receptive to it. The force does not come from me, but rather it comes through me, and the more I am receptive to it, the more my life flows and the more my music flows.' The more laconic Thomson adds that the more 'childlike' in his perceptions he can become, the better music he can make."

"After the interview, Benson explains that since the station manager wants to avoid the appearance of the station providing free advertising for the band, the interview will not be on the air until after the concert that evening. Since this is the band's first visit to Pittsburgh and advance ticket sales have been only about seven thousand, this is not good news, but the group takes it in its stride."

Still from the same feature; "'It looks lust like a giant breast', remarks Prevost, back in the car as they circle the Civic Arena looking for an entrance to the backstage. It is 5:30pm when the musicians enter the hall for their sound check. The forty foot stage and the sound system is already in place, and all that is needed are a few last minute corrections before the show can go on. Unlike many major rock acts which find it more convenient and economical to lease the elaborate sound systems needed for an arena tour, Supertramp, via its Delicate Acoustics sound company, owns its own. The system, which weighs about twenty six tonnes and is insured for more than five million dollars, is rented out to other acts when Supertramp is not on the road. It was used by Kansas last year. Sitting in a small backstage room, surrounded by Helliwell's woodwinds, Ian Lloyd-Bisley, the electrician on the tour who also handles the monitors, gives some of the specs. Though as sophisticated as any, the Supertramp sound and light system is not as overwhelmingly powerful as some, and the band does not need an extra generator to travel with it, it uses local power sources. While the sound and light crews are making their last minute adjustments and the security force and ushers are being briefed on their duties, a local caterer supplied by the promoter, prepares food for the hungry. Meanwhile, the five principals of the band are onstage making their own preparations to ensure that once they get before an audience there will be no hang-ups. It is a singularly relaxed atmosphere with Helliwell reading out loud from an advice column parody in *Punch* magazine before he is attacked and playfully wrestled to the ground by Hodgson and Thomson. Davies, at stage left, fusses with his keyboards, informing one of the roadies that the instrument needs cleaning because the keys are beginning to stick. Another roadie is sanding down the sharp rims of the heavy ends of Benberg's drum sticks."

"By 6:30, an hour before the show is to begin, the stage is ready and the musicians retire to their sparse but not unclean dressing rooms, affording an opportunity to chat with them. Why, they are asked, when such acts as Yes, Genesis and Emerson, Lake and Palmer, which all play a similar form of English art rock, are finding themselves on the cut-out racks, is Supertramp right there on top? 'Well, there is a distinct lack of anything else around now', offers Hodgson, 'there is more fun and warmth on this LP, and at the same time the humour is offset by the seriousness of some of the lyrics. We sometimes joke that if we really wanted to be commercial, we could clean up.' 'I really don't know why this LP has been so popular, but I can tell you it has given encouragement to a lot of people', says Benberg, reflecting the uncertainty that is beginning to nag some of the established bands who may be wondering if they haven't grown out of date. 'Musically it (*Breakfast In America*) is pretty commercial', says the laconic and thoughtful Rick Davies, who looks and sounds a little like a bearded John Lennon onstage (he probably hates the comparison) 'There are short compact songs, quite melodic, that's combined with the timing of the tour, a lot of success with the single ('The Logical Song')... It has done better than one would expect it to.' Davies seems uncomfortable with even this brief interview and wanders off to play darts with the other band members. There is a dart board set up in the hallway just outside the dressing rooms. Darts has become a preshow ritual. 'Just before a show even don't try to talk to him', says Davies' wife Sue. Where the husband is almost shy, the wife, a former publicity and artist development executive with A&M Records, has no hesitation talking about her business. Selling Supertramp T-shirts, tour books, and baseball jerseys is hard work and a constant battle that can explode into real violence with bootleggers, says Sue Davies who has been known to personally confront the wrongdoers out in the parking lots. On nights such as this, when there is no bootleg problem, the merchandising business can be quite profitable with the band grossing about one dollar twenty five per head from concert going fans. The halls get a thirty to forty percent commission on this, and in some places, like Madison Square Garden, the hall takes half, says Sue Davies. There are many ways to try to control merchandising bootleggers, she adds, none of them wholly satisfactory. Some bands take the law into their own hands, with the security forces attempting to confiscate the merchandise; that is not really legal and can lead to serious problems. What she tries to do, she says, is to work with the hall in hiring police to arrest the bootleggers for trespassing or for peddling without a license or not paying the local sales taxes. For a travelling band to attempt to get a court injunction to block the bootleggers over copyright infringement is almost impossible to do because of the time involved in instituting civil court proceedings, and the proof needed. In addition to worrying about bootleggers, who are worst in the Northeast, she says, there is always the problem of keeping up supplies while on the road, which in this age of truck strikes and gas shortages, is not the easiest to do. Though Prevost remarks on the comeliness of some of the fans (Pittsburgh is known on the road for its good looking women), what he is really looking for is the presence of any tape recorders. He says there is a clause in the Supertramp contract with promoters that holds the promoters liable for up to 500,000 dollars should a bootleg album appear which was recorded within their venues."

"The five Supertramp musicians take their places behind a black screen and the show begins at 7:50pm. The band plays a clean and precise set, which is melodic and slightly jazzy, with a hint of the Beatles, but the music is never too self indulgent, and the musicians look much more relaxed and like they are having fun than during the band's visit to Madison Square Garden a week earlier. As the music continues so do the stage effects, some quite good, as a speeded up film of a train trip projected on a screen from the back of the stage, and some just silly, as when a roadie dressed as a gorilla in a waitress's uniform dances with another roadie made up to look as a giant banana. Prevost explains that the band has been using these effects for quite a while now, and it has become a tradition with the band that the member of the crew with the least seniority gets the dubious distinction of being the gorilla. Through it all, the larger than expected audience is well behaved and appreciative of the music. The kids cheer the songs they know and stay respectful and in their seats during some of the quieter sequences. The band earns a well-deserved encore, and by 9:55pm the show is over. The music, the staging, and the crystal clear sound have all contributed to a successful gig. Right after the concert the musicians retire to their dressing rooms to change, relax and catch their breaths, before emerging about forty-five minutes later, in the backstage area, while the stage is already being torn down. From the hall it's back to the nearby hotel via a mode of transportation rarely employed by rock stars — by foot. On the way, Thomson says he doesn't mind life on the road at all. In fact the bass player says that after the tour he is thinking of getting a house trailer and travelling around the US on his own. But what he really wants, he says, is a house boat he can live and travel on. Back at the hotel there are a few fans around, but nothing like the scene the Saturday night before when groupies roamed the halls of the Hyatt House looking for members of Journey. Supertramp appears to attract a bit more serious, or at least more reserved, devotees. The musicians go to their rooms, but soon reconvene at the hotel bar for a nightcap. At the bar, Rick and Sue Davies huddle with promoter Richard Engler, while Roger Hodgson makes a surprise brief appearance to get some mineral water for his wife Karuna, who arrived with their baby during the evening from Indianapolis. The Hodgson's usually travel together by trailer but for this leg they decided to take a vacation from driving. By noon, the band and its entourage is on the way out of the hotel and, unlike on their arrival, some of the musicians are recognised and asked for their autographs. And then it's out the door, and into cabs, for another city and another show."

Wow! What an eventful day and then some! Although in and of itself it perhaps doesn't sound like too much, to do the same thing day in, day out with all the travelling and lack of alone time involved, it is understandable as to why the *Breakfast In America* tour was such that the band were keen to have a well earned rest afterwards. It's fascinating to learn of the clever incentives the tour organisers employed to encourage each venue to be vigilant for concert goers trying to smuggle in tape recorders for the purpose of bootlegging. Clever but slightly annoying as in, from a fan's perspective, who doesn't love a good bootleg? They're not to everyone's taste I suppose but they can certainly offer an insight into what any band sounds like live and unedited. It's a long article but I have included the whole thing here in this book because as a first hand account of a day in the life of Supertramp during the *Breakfast In America* tour, it really gets across the extent to which the band was in such demand at the time.

The intensity of Supertramp's schedule at the time of *Breakfast In America* was well explained by journalist, Harry Doherty, in June 1979 in *Melody Maker*; "Another essential ingredient in the arrival of Supertramp was and is undoubtedly the gruelling touring pattern to which the band has adhered to ever since its inception. When they record, the band sink into studio life for months. As a result, they're left with huge world tours to undertake. When they go out on the road, it's never a half measure. This is not the first nine-month tour on which Supertramp have embarked but the weight of endless one-nighters has taken its toll. This will, in fact, be Supertramp's last major tour — one of the few areas where Rick Davies and Roger Hodgson find themselves in total agreement. The decision it seems, has already been taken. Both writers are acutely aware of the need to slow down, so that their joint and separate creativity may develop to its full potential."

In the feature, Rick was quoted; "I think we're going to have to use the time a little more creatively than just endless tours because that will kill us in the end. We have to figure that one out." Doherty added; "Dougie Thomson strategically points out that Supertramp are caught up in the commercial circle of touring-recording-touring and acknowledges with regret that it is a tight grip to break. Actually it might seem surprising that Supertramp should have such a strong reputation as a touring band. By rights they should be considered primarily a studio band with secondary touring interests, which would allow them the space to breathe creatively. But that's not the case, and Davies is particularly desperate to crack the system, hoping that they might do condensed tours in the future."

Rick was quoted as he considered how he felt his writing had suffered from doing all the touring; "The five songs that I did on *Breakfast In America* are the only things I've done in three years. I can't think straight when we're on the road. I'm just thinking about where we're going next. The problem is that three of the band are not writers. It's up to them to find their little niches, for when the band aren't touring. It's down to 'can we survive without being around each other so much? Can we all exist within our own little worlds and then come back together as Supertramp?' It's difficult because John loves to tour. He loves to play more than anything else whereas I'm ready to go home. I feel bad for him. It's a question of being able to handle that."

Similarly, it comes across that Roger Hodgson had had enough of touring by this point too, as he was quoted in the same feature; "Touring agrees with me less and less now. I think this is the last one for me. It's probably the last one for all of us. There's more things to life. I still want to play to people because that's in a musician's blood, but in a way I get as much, probably even more, playing an acoustic guitar in front of a room full of people than I do getting up there in front of 15,000 people. I get much more reward within myself. It's totally different but I prefer the intimacy which you just totally lose when you play these places. It's a show. I feel like I'm part of a show. I don't feel I'm me. But in a room full of people you know that every single subtlety will be picked up. Artistically, our show is like a play. We go out and do the same play every night, maybe slightly different depending on how you feel and how you vibe with the actors. That's how I see us now. It's like an experience that people come and see. That's the biggest motivation, that people do want to see it, and I really believe that it's one of the best rock shows that's ever been. But as far as my life goes, I don't feel that it's expanding me musically or artistically. It's my job, basically, at the moment. It's something we've got to do in order to earn ourselves the freedom to develop artistically, which means coming off the road. I'm feeling very clear about this in my mind. I don't think we can do much more with the songs. We've done it. The show is as good as it can be. All we could do now with the music we've got and the songs and the lighting is get bigger and better, and there's no point really because we don't want to get any bigger than this. By the end of this tour, it'll be time to move on. Rick said something once about the Beatles, that their most creative period came when they stopped touring. That might have been coincidence. It might have been LSD. But I think there's a great truth in that. Touring is a very unreal world. You haven't got your feet on the ground. It's funny, but although I have a great belief in the show, I won't miss it when we stop."

Hodgson was quoted in the Canadian paper, *The Standard* in December 2008; "Even though we were fortunate that our rise to mega-success was gradual, it was still an intense adjustment when *Breakfast In America* hit it so big. It was number one worldwide for almost half a year and has sold for decades. I think everyone dealt with fame, success and wealth differently. I always say it's a hot fire to go through — it's anything but the glamorous picture that people imagine it to be. There are a lot of casualties. There were many lessons and experiences I had to go through to regain my perspective on life. I'm grateful to have always had a passionate yearning to know God, to know love and to be of service. The biggest thing I learned from all the fame and success is how they are not keys to happiness. Usually the opposite, in fact. I do believe though, that the more life gives you, the more you have to give back and it's in the giving back that you will find fulfilment and purpose."

It really seems that Hodgson did not enjoy himself in the *Breakfast In America* days of the band in some ways. He was quoted in September 1983 in *Jam* as he explained candidly on the matter; "Up until *Breakfast In America*, there really were magical feelings when writing and recording Supertramp material. We had a very close kind of family feeling for a long, long time really, up until *Breakfast In America*. *Breakfast* is really where it started diverging and everyone started looking outside the Supertramp music for their personal happiness and fulfilment."

On balance though, Hodgson also clarified, "I am very, very happy that it did happen. It is a great album. It wasn't really so much the album; it was the nine-month marathon tour that followed it. We did one hundred and twenty shows in nine months and almost killed ourselves and killed the band as well. It was during that tour really

that the songs began to sound very, very tired and very, very old. I felt like I needed to do something else and probably should have gone and made the decision to leave straight after that tour at the end of '79. However, it wasn't the time to talk after the tour."

The whole thing of trying to balance family life with life on the road was pretty much evident in a number of media reports at the time, particularly concerning Hodgson. In *Melody Maker* in June 1979, his presence in the featured interview is introduced in a way that portrays a man who is trying his best to multitask; "It's 2AM in the car park of the Cleveland Coliseum and the fan belt on Roger Hodgson's motor home has just snapped. We're stranded. And the baby's crying. And Roger wants to talk about the psychic powers of music. He has a captive audience."

It was even the case that said baby was born during the tour itself. *Cash Box* reported in April 1979; "Roger Hodgson and his wife Karuna had a baby girl, the couple's first, last Wednesday in San Diego. Amazingly, Karuna gave birth to the baby in a mobile home in the parking lot of the San Diego Sports Arena, just twelve minutes before the group was scheduled to take the stage. Weighing in at seven pounds and fourteen ounces, the baby girl (who is yet to be named) and mother are both doing well."

In May 1979, *Record World* reported their version of events; "Supertramp has always prided itself on appearing on stage on time. For those who wondered why the band was thirty-four minutes late for its April 11th San Diego date, the answer arrived from road manager Bob Roper via postcard (aka portable press release). It seems that Roger and Karuna Hodgson received a seven pound, four ounce female gift from above just before showtime. Although they tried to make it to a local hospital, Karuna gave birth in the mobile home in the hospital parking lot."

Roger was quoted in *Melody Maker* in June 1979; "This child has come into the world to teach me how to be a child again, rather than me teach her how to be an adult. I don't want to teach her how to be an adult. I just want to rediscover the fun and joy that little kids have naturally, and that we all have really. There should be fun in everything."

Roger was quoted in *Jam* in September 1983 as he explained with candour that the wealth that came with the success of *Breakfast In America* was actually something that he found quite alienating and was something that brought a new set of stresses to the table; "Money had a lot to do with the attitude change in Supertramp. In fact, it changes your attitude about a lot of things. From thinking in terms of the band, once we achieved success with *Breakfast In America*, we took some time off, and it was the first time that we had a chance to have a home life and get into our own individual lives. We started thinking individually rather than as a collective band. I think that the biggest challenge an artist can have is success, and especially financial success, because money brings with it a whole different set of challenges. It is very easy for it to consume you, not only in how you are going to spend it, but it takes a lot of looking after. Before you know it, it really does control your life time wise. Financial independence is very, very difficult to master. You just don't have any time for anything else. You tend to want to buy your own house, move away from a life, the lifestyle of the people you sing to. You kind of isolate yourself and lose touch with the way people you sing to are feeling from day to day. It is very easy for you to lose your perspective and I think for us, money really did that."

It is fascinating that after Sam withdrew funding from Supertramp, they had gone from rags to riches, from a struggling band (where some members had to hold down day jobs too) to supergroup status and yet, it still didn't seem to provide a full sense of joy and achievement. Roger Hodgson certainly has a way of describing things that makes you think!

For Hodgson, the hiatus from the band consisted of him moving with his family from the Los Angeles area to the mountains of California. He built a home and studio there in order to focus on family, spirituality

and recording a solo album. The album's working title was *Sleeping With The Enemy* but it was ultimately released as *Eye Of The Storm* in 1984. It is considered by some that Hodgson's geographic separation from the rest of the band was not conducive for the next album but still, after *Breakfast In America*, it really does seem that everyone probably needed a rest anyway.

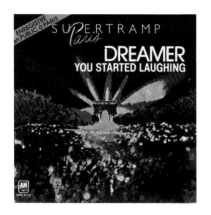

THURS. APR. 19 - 8 PM
MEMORIAL COLISEUM

RESERVED SEAT TICKETS: $7/$7.50/$8.00
AVAILABLE: MEIER & FRANK, EVERYBODY'S RECORDS,
ALL G.I. JOES (BEAVERTON, N. PORTLAND, OAK GROVE,
ROCKWOOD, & EASTPORT - VISA & MASTERCHARGE
ACCEPTED), PENDULUM IN VANCOUVER, THE
MALE BAG IN HILLSBORO, & THE COLISEUM BOX
OFFICE.

Supertramp at Memorial Coliseum, Portland, Oregon, 19th April 1979.

Chapter Eight:
...Famous Last Words... (1982)

"...famous last words..."

Seemingly, the success of *Breakfast In America* had caused a change in dynamics within the band. As Hodgson was quoted in *Classic Rock Revisited* in February 2012; "There were a lot of other things also happening. On the *Breakfast In America* tour I had my first child. Shortly afterward, I had my second child and suddenly I had a family. Other band members were also going through a lot of changes like that. I have always tried to follow my heart and my instincts in life. When I made the decision to leave the band, three years later, it was because my heart was telling me to stop because I needed to learn how to be a father. I was wanting to step away from the music business for a while in order to have a more simple lifestyle. This was at the peak of Supertramp's success, so it was a difficult decision but I just knew I had to do it in order to be at home with my children as they grew up. Supertramp had been my baby. It had been my passion for fourteen years but my heart was telling me that this was more important than to continue with Supertramp at that time. Looking back, I do not regret my decision. My kids have grown up and I was able to learn a lot and give to them while they were growing up. I believe my absence from the music business at that time is why I am still in my prime, creatively, today."

The intensity of the *Breakfast In America* tour was such that it had taken its toll on Rick and Roger's writing partnership. Hope that the rapport could be repaired was definitely there and I would argue that that is largely why *...Famous Last Words...* exists. Roger was quoted in *Melody Maker* in June 1979 regarding the impact that touring was having on him and indeed on the writing partnership; "I think we both really need to have a break, just to step back from everything and look at it. I think we both feel that we want to work closer together again, because that's really where the magic happens. We haven't had the opportunity to write together or jam together in a room for five years. I guess it's our own fault. For a start, you have to want to and I guess there's been so much other stuff filling our heads and minds that we just haven't had the time. Hopefully, the success of this album (*Breakfast In America*) has given us time to do that. Rick and I are really starved of musical growth. We've climbed to the top of the mountain. Now what do we do? Most bands just stay at the top and sing the same old songs, but that means nothing to us. We really feel like we've got to grow. The band will stay together as long as it's growing. If it's reached a peak, we might as well find other musicians and do something else."

All good things in life come to an end and after the dizzying highs from the success of *Breakfast In America*, Supertramp's next album, *...Famous Last Words...* is certainly symptomatic of that, not necessarily musically but certainly in terms of the dynamic between Davies and Hodgson by that time. The writing process for *...Famous Last Words...* was a challenge for both men because it was felt by the rest of the band that Hodgson wanted out and it was during the world tour for the album in 1983 that Hodgson announced that he would be leaving Supertramp. He maintained that his reasons weren't due to any major personal or professional problems with the band and that his decision was based on a need to spend more time with his family and grow his ideas and projects as a solo artist.

...Famous Last Words..., Supertramp's seventh studio album, was therefore their last with the classic Hodgson, Davies, Helliwell, Thomson and Siebenberg line-up. The album was released in October 1982. It got to number five in America and number six in the UK where it was certified gold for the sale of 100,000 copies. The album also spanned hit singles with 'It's Raining Again' and 'My Kind Of Lady'. Hodgson was quoted in the *North County Times* in February 2011; "'It's Raining Again' came pouring out of me one day. I was at my mother's house and had just lost a friend. It was raining outside, and I was feeling melancholy and sat down to play my harmonium. It's a sad

song with an upbeat melody."

In the same interview, he elaborated, "My songwriting process has never changed, I've always written songs when I'm alone, not with a band. I have always found it very difficult to be in composing mode around other people. For me it is a very personal process, usually late at night when I find myself alone and I can really tune in. Generally, the music comes first with a few lines of lyrics, then for a two or three week period of time I sing the song every opportunity I get. I usually hear every note in my head first and slowly the lyrics take shape. When it's complete I make a demo. I would then bring the complete demo to the band to learn their parts."

The single, 'It's Raining Again', was reviewed in *Billboard* in October 1982; "Roger Hodgson's airy lead vocal serves notice that Supertramp is back after a three year hiatus and pop, AOR and AC will be quick to welcome them via this lush mid-tempo charmer. John Helliwell's soaring sax lines and a sing-song children's chorus at the fade are the icing on the cake."

'It's Raining Again' was reviewed in *Cash Box* in October 1982; "The first single from the long awaited ...*Famous Last Words*... LP, this is vintage Supertramp with all of the elements that have made the group's sound so distinctive. Bouncy and hook-laden, this up-tempo number, featuring the floating vocals of Roger Hodgson, should brighten up any playlist. The top debut this week on the pop chart."

Billboard reviewed 'My Kind Of Lady' in January 1983; "To follow the top twenty 'It's Raining Again', Supertramp goes 1956 to the Platters/Presley/Satins era of chunky piano, bleating sax and rhymes you can quote before you've heard them. The group's sense of fun wins out as usual in this second release from ...*Famous Last Words*... ."

Hodgson was quoted in the *St Louis Post Dispatch* in May 1998 as he explained some of the emotional process he experienced in wanting to go solo; "I'd been trying to maybe find myself outside of myself. When you're in a band you almost lose your identity. I put fourteen years of my life into building Supertramp and then suddenly it wasn't there anymore and there was a huge vacuum. It took me a while to realise that the vacuum needed to be filled by myself. I immediately went to see Steve Winwood after I left Supertramp because I needed to find another partner. But the partner I've needed to find is just myself. When I feel complete in myself then I can work with anyone."

The creation of ...*Famous Last Words*... was unique in terms of how it was the first Supertramp album where Davies and Hodgson didn't conceive the overall theme for the album together. As a result, there was much disagreement between the two with regards to what direction to take the band and the album in by this point. Hodgson wanted to make another pop album similar to *Breakfast In America* and Davies wanted to do a progressive rock album that included a ten minute song called 'Brother Where You Bound' as the centrepiece. Bob Siebenberg considered that due to the strong artistic differences between Hodgson and Davies, it resulted in the ...*Famous Last Words*... album being a diluted project based on compromise all round that nobody was really that happy with.

The division in the band is perhaps even evident in the sleeve notes of the album whereby a colour code system was used to connate who had done what writing on each song in terms of lyrics and music. Most of …*Famous Last Words…* was recorded and mixed at Hodgson's home, Unicorn Studios in California. This was apparently due to him wanting to be close to his wife and young children. Davies recorded his part for the album at his home studio, The Backyard Studios, also in California. All other overdubs for the album were done at Bill Schnee Recording Studios in Los Angeles.

In *Jam* in September 1983, Roger was quoted as he spoke candidly about how he had had enough of feeling that he had to make albums with Rick under contractual obligations; "We are at a point now where Rick and myself, the two writers, the two forces within the band, where for many reasons, we kind of need to get divorced before we can be friends again. That is what I call it. It's not working being tied to each other contractually and having to make albums rather than make albums because we want to. I am certainly open for the future. Maybe three or four years down the line, we will feel like working together. But, at the moment, it is pretty clear that we need to go and spread our wings." Fair enough as in, if something feels obligatory rather than organic, it is understandable as to how this wouldn't be helpful for anyone's creative process.

John Helliwell offered some insight into Hodgson's departure when he was quoted in *Cash Box* in February 1988; "With Roger and Rick writing the numbers, and Supertramp making an album every couple of years or so, each writer had four songs every two years. Roger was so prolific, he had a library of thirty to fifty songs or more and he wasn't getting his material out. He could have continued and done a solo album on the side but ever since *Breakfast In America* he was hankering to leave really. He thought Supertramp had run its course, while we didn't. When he left, the other band members had a choice of calling it a day or carrying on with Rick. We felt the band was still a viable and valid entity."

Hodgson was quoted in September 1983 in *Jam*; "We took two years off and got back together again, did another album …*Famous Last Words…*, to see if it would work again. It didn't. Really, it comes down to what is happening in one's life at the time an album is recorded as to whether a project is magical or it's not. *Breakfast In America* was magical, *Crime Of The Century* was magical. The albums that are successes really stem from having a good time making them. There are a set of circumstances that make for a chemistry that makes magic, and I think that that is the main ingredient. You can never tell when that is going to happen."

It really comes across that the classic line-up had really had enough of working together by that point. No more chemistry. No more magic. Hold that thought though, it's not all doom and gloom and whilst Roger Hodgson was weighing up his future with Supertramp whilst on hiatus post *Breakfast In America*, it seems that not everyone had such an intense time away from the band.

In November 1982, *Record Mirror* offered an unusually detailed insight into some of the band's life outside of music. It was reported; "It's a life on the ocean wave for

AT LAST
FAMOUS WORDS
FROM
SUPERTRAMP
FAMOUS
SUPERTRAMP
WORDS
AT LAST
THE WORD
FROM
SUPERTRAMP
AT LAST

FAMOUS LAST WORDS
The new studio album from
SUPERTRAMP

1 WEEK TO GO

Supertramp, currently continuing the aquatic theme in the singles chart with 'It's Raining' (sic). Dougie Thomson, their thirty-one-year-old Glaswegian bass player, actually lives on a boat off the California coast. During Supertramp's eighteen-month hiatus he used it to travel the Pacific coastline down to Mexico. Last year he journeyed over 10,000 miles."

In the same piece, Dougie was quoted; "I think it's something in my blood, I used to go down to the Clyde with my grandfather as a kid to go on day trips on the big steamers. Despite what people say about the Clyde, it was pretty romantic to me. Our family also had a caravan in Dunbar, near Edinburgh on the east coast of Scotland. I can remember going down to watch the fishing boats coming in. I spent loads of time hanging around the harbour. Some of the skippers would take me out for a few hours. I always used to wonder what it would be like to have an adventure."

Thomson certainly found out what such adventure was like. The feature includes the fact that at the time, he owned a forty-four single masted sloop with two cabins. His seamanship was predominantly self-taught, but he did go to night school to get his navigation certificate. He was quoted; "There's a lot of hard work, not just to sail it but to maintain it. Saltwater is a destroyer of everything and sun just makes it worse. There's always something to fix. It gets hairy from time to time. I've been in force nine — that's fifty knots of wind — with twenty foot waves. I go scuba diving a lot so I usually set sail for places where the underwater scenery is beautiful. The first time I saw a shark I was scared shitless. I was only about three feet away from it. It was only a nurse shark — it only feeds on plankton — but I couldn't tell at that time who were the good guys and who were the bad. I once saw a ten-foot lemon shark. I was about five feet behind it. One of my companions swam up to it and whacked it across the tail and he took off. A pal of mine just got bitten. It was a small black tip shark. It bit him on his leg. Luckily he had his knife strapped across his calf so it couldn't bite right through. It still ripped through the tendons in his calf and he had to have a couple of operations. He's alright now. In fact, he was back in the water within three weeks."

Luckily, Thomson remained undeterred as he continued in response to the interviewer's joke that he could become a true life victim for *Jaws Three*; "You have a better chance of getting run over… Sailing gives me a good balance so that when I come back to Supertramp I'm raring to go and enthusiastic."

In the same feature, Bob Siebenberg was quoted on his enjoyment of the aquatic lifestyle; "I go surfing most weekends so I like being on the ocean. I think there are more people in the water than ever. The only reason it doesn't seem as big is because the Beach Boys don't sing about it anymore. The romance is still there. I still believe that the only way to see a sunset is from a surfboard." Cowabunga! Or something like that anyway.

Admittedly, transcribing this article was fascinating and amusing in equal measure as in, here we have a band who are generally renowned for not being particularly outspoken about their life outside of music and yet, this article is very rare in how it gets right down to the specifics. I certainly never expected to be thinking about life at sea (or the equivalent water related thing depending on location) whilst thinking about Supertramp!

At the time of the album's release, Hodgson was yet to announce his planned departure from the band. Due to the fact that the title of the album fuelled the rumour that it would be Supertramp's last, Helliwell sought to discourage such rumours at the time by insisting that the meaning of the album's title was actually embedded in the concept of enigma. Not the best explanation perhaps but fair play for trying.

It comes across that there was no animosity in the split after the ...Famous Last Words... album. Hodgson was quoted in February 2012 in Classic Rock Revisited; "It was more a natural breakup. In a way, ...Famous Last Words... was an attempt to give it one more shot and it didn't work. The album had a hit and it did very well, but for me, artistically, it was very disappointing. It was the same way for Rick. We called the album ...Famous Last Words... because we didn't want to go through that again. It was all happening at the same time. The band was falling apart and people were going their separate directions. For me, I wanted to be with my family and to be committed to that."

Seemingly, the desire to leave Supertramp was upon Hodgson even in the early stages of working on ...Famous Last Words... and if not, even prior to that. Ever the philosopher, in the same interview, Hodgson continued, "When you're in the music industry you can lose sight of things very easily. I had to pull back and see what my priorities were and what was important to me. My heart was not into it and I had to make a change. At a certain point, my heart was telling me that it was over and that the journey was over with Supertramp. I had to let go of the baby I had created. It was very difficult but it was very necessary and it opened up a phase of my life's journey that has been very, very important to me." It was announced in Cash Box in March 1983 that "Roger Hodgson will leave Supertramp at the end of the group's summer tour."

When he was quoted in The San Diego Union Tribune in February 2011, Hodgson was keen to assert that his main motive for leaving was not embedded in the need to have a solo career and that it was much more about wanting to focus on other things in his life. Whilst he did get a solo career up and running after leaving the band, it is possibly the case that this could have been as a side effect of simply being in the habit of wanting to make music; "When I left Supertramp in 1983 it was to follow my heart, which was telling me it was time to make home, family and spiritual life my priority. I wanted to be with my children as they grew up. I chose to have my primary focus be my family and not my career. I also pretty much left the music industry and took my family to a healthier place to raise my kids in — up the mountains of Northern California. I moved out of Los Angeles and built a home studio so I could continue to create music, and although I made a few albums, I never toured behind them. Contrary to what people believed, Supertramp did not break up because I wanted to start a solo career or because of difficulties between Rick and I."

Hodgson was quoted in The Sunday Times in July 1983; "Making our last album,

...*Famous Last Words*... took sixteen months, which was an emotionally difficult time. We were sick of listening to the songs after four months. It was an awful strain. We had already gone our separate ways when we decided to have one more try with the last album. It didn't work. I call it a divorce. Rick and I had learned as much as we could from each other. We've always had a strange relationship — a deep love for each other — but we're different characters." Yeah, it doesn't seem that Rick and Roger not wanting to work together anymore was based on hate or a falling out, it simply seems that creatively and in terms of musical chemistry, the partnership had run out of mileage.

In May 1983, *Billboard* reported on Supertramp's upcoming tour; "Supertramp is currently setting off on its last world tour as the five-man band its fans have come to know. Before Roger Hodgson leaves the group, it plans to make one enormous last hurrah. There will be twenty-eight shows on the European leg of the tour — all but two of them outdoors — in seven weeks, followed by thirty dates in the US throughout August and September. Due to the tight scheduling of the performances, two complete stages are being built so that one can be set up while the second is being used. The cost of the equipment Supertramp is bringing along exceeds five million dollars."

Stage manager Ian Lloyd-Bisley was quoted, "The stage has to be physically large because of the amount of PA we use. Each metal structure is one hundred and sixty feet by forty-six feet. But the stage is relatively clear and clean, rather simple compared to, say, Rod Stewart's... We're going to need fifteen or sixteen trucks (and) four coaches. It will take twenty-five people just to put the metal up. Then there will be twelve people on the sound crew, eight on the light crew and six on the stage crew, a lot of people to feed. A show like this is much more difficult in Europe than in America because of the language barrier and the different power standards. You sometimes have to go through two sets of customs guards in a single day, and the potential for trouble is always there. The power difference creates the worst problems. A stagehand was almost electrocuted on the last tour because of it."

Another exciting feature of the tour was that an additional two musicians, Scott Page and Fred Mandel were to be on stage in order to allow Supertramp to perform songs that wouldn't otherwise be possible live. 'Gone Hollywood' is one of the songs that was made possible in the live set via the addition of two more musicians. In the same article, Lloyd-Bisley was also quoted; "Roger leaving the band will change things. It will be good for him, and it will also revitalise the rest of the band. There will be a new member, maybe two. It won't really hit me that it's happened until the last show at the Forum in LA. In the meantime, this show is going to be powerful. People are going to get their money's worth."

On balance, as much as Hodgson made it abundantly clear to the rest of the band, and eventually, the public that he had had enough of being in Supertramp and was not happy with the ...*Famous Last Words*... album, it is worth remembering that in the live shows, Supertramp were still on top of their game, at least as they appeared to Derek Jewell who reviewed one of their live shows in the *Daily Express* on 13th July

1983; "Waiting for Supertramp seems to have been a pastime of flash-rockers since time was much younger. It took them six years to break through with *Crime Of The Century* in 1974. It's taken them three-and-a-half years to get on the road again. And they were an hour late at Earl's Court on Wednesday when a 17,000 trance of the million who are seeing them this time around were in ecstasy at their spectacular two-hour reincarnation. Pomp rock dead? Don't make me laugh. Pomp is alive and burning as the near-certainty that a ticket promising a support band would turn out not to deliver — unless the 'support' was the piano-tuner who appeared at 8.40, and the unedifying sight of roadies swarming up rope-ladders. Still, when Super T (sic) finally made it, they gave superb value. With seven musicians a-playing, and the heart of the band — lead singers Dick Davies (sic) and the departing Roger Hodgson, with reeds player John Helliwell — in great form, the symphonic synthesised extravaganzas and the neat, sharp, brittle quickies like 'Dreamer' and 'Logical Song' (sic) kept a-rolling juggernaut-fashion. The show was framed in a splendidly pyrotechnic set — lights used with arty bombast and the film clips were diverting, if seldom inspiring, except for the sudden sight of Churchill declaiming, 'We shall defend our island — we shall never surrender', during the powerful climax. This statement was as wildly cheered as finally were Supertramp, an indication perhaps that the factions of pomp and punk are as deeply divided as they keep telling us England is; and that, in the end, pomp rules as Margaret Thatcher does."

Admittedly, I'm not a fan of how the reviewer calls Rick, Dick Davies. Nor am I a fan of how the reviewer felt the need to call the band Super T and refer to the music as pomp rock and compare Supertramp to Margaret Thatcher. Still though, the reviewer didn't ask me (I wasn't there man!) and the point is this; even whilst the classic line-up of Supertramp was just months away from breaking up, they were still on top of their game in the live arena where their classic songs were being enjoyed by large audience numbers.

Supertramp's live show at Brendan Byrne Arena, Meadowlands in New Jersey was reviewed in *Billboard* in September 1983; "Since they burst onto the rock scene in 1974 with *Crime Of The Century*, Supertramp has been regarded as one of the most professional and talented bands around. The group's 9th August trip to New Jersey Byrne Arena was the band's 'farewell' visit before founding member Roger Hodgson departs Supertramp to embark on a solo career. In a stunning rock show, Supertramp seemed to reach back for something extra and rendered a truly unforgettable performance. The members of Supertramp — Hodgson, Rick Davies, John Helliwell, Dougie Thomson and Bob Siebenberg — take the music very seriously and play with the seasoned cool of master musicians. Hodgson's abilities are so overwhelming it's somewhat staggering. Besides being the composer of some of the band's biggest hits, he also sings and plays keyboards and guitar. It was Roger who visibly moved the audience when he walked to the microphone and announced, 'This is a very special tour for Supertramp. At the end of this tour, I'll be leaving, but if the music grows, then it's good. I'd like to take this opportunity to thank everyone who's given us so much support over the years, and this is my song for you.' With that said, Hodgson and the band broke into one of their biggest hits, 'Give A Little Bit'. Later in the evening, Hodgson remarked, 'This song is for all of you who have avoided becoming vegetables.' Right on cue, the band broke into 'The Logical Song'. One could close his eyes and swear the record was being piped in via the PA system. Supertramp's ability to reproduce their sound in a concert situation is nothing short of extraordinary. Their set was chock full of hits and included 'Goodbye Stranger', 'Dreamer', 'Bloody Well Right', 'It's Raining Again' and a stunning version of 'Fool's Overture'. It is difficult for this observer to believe the loss of Roger Hodgson will not severely impact on his band's popularity. Nonetheless, the group's 'farewell tour' with Hodgson is an event unto itself and should not be missed by anyone who cares about rock 'n' roll."

The good reviews of live shows during the time of the ...*Famous Last Words*... album are certainly consistent. Genuinely. I'll show you another one. This one is from the *St Louis Post Dispatch* and was reviewed by Louise King on 15th September 1983; "Mixed emotions filled the Checkerdome amphitheatre on Wednesday night. Supertramp fans were overjoyed to see the band play here for the first time in more than eight years, but reluctant to say goodbye to lead singer/keyboard player/guitarist Roger Hodgson, who is leaving the group after fourteen years to pursue a solo career. Supertramp's current tour, the final one with its present line-up, marks the end of an era in rock music. The group went out as it came in — with style. The quintet has spared nothing in putting together its most spectacular show to date. To that end, the instrumental and vocal artistry of Hodgson, lead singer/keyboard player Rick Davies, reedman John Helliwell, bassist Dougie Thomson and drummer Bob C. Benberg has been supplemented by two multitalented performers. As a studio musician, Fred Mandel worked with stars like Diana Ross and Queen before joining the Supertramp tour. The Toronto native played keyboards and delivered a scorching guitar solo on 'Don't Leave Me Now'. Scott Page, who hails from Los Angeles, found plenty to keep him occupied as he juggled guitar, sax, keyboard and percussion duties throughout the evening. Both contributed to the vocals as well. The addition of Mandel and Page had the intended effect — it filled gaps previously left in the live instrumental arrangements and freed the remaining members to concentrate on the vocal performance. The music was augmented, but never dominated by a series of splendid special effects, including three huge light tripods suspended over the stage and video clips periodically displayed on a mammoth screen above the crowd. Twice during the show members of the road crew appeared in costume to highlight a particular song. From the start, the differences that have finally brought songwriters Hodgson and Davies to a parting of the ways were obvious. The show opened with Hodgson's 'Crazy', from the 1982 release, ...*Famous Last Words*... as the album's cover art was brought to life on the video screen. The bright, up tempo tune is perfectly suited to Hodgson's light, spirited tenor, while Davies' funkier voice matched the moodiness of the next song, 'Ain't Nobody But Me', featuring the dual saxophones of Helliwell and Page. In the end, it was primarily Hodgson's songs that stirred the crowd. Ovation after ovation was heaped upon the familiar 'Breakfast In America', 'It's Raining Again', 'The Logical Song' and 'Dreamer'. But at no time was the emotion greater than when Hodgson, usually a non-talker on stage, shared his feeling about this final tour, and offered 'Give A Little Bit' to thank everyone for the love shown to him over the years. The show had many highlights, including the audience's visual train ride via the video screen during 'Rudy' and the full-length climactic performance of 'Fool's Overture'. The latter featured a unique blend of pretty vocals and strong rhythms, skilfully woven around a tightly choreographed combination of video clips, sound and lighting effects and unusual costumes. Only encores like 'School' and 'Crime Of The Century' could follow it. As the crowd took its final video voyage of the evening this time to outer space, Supertramp took its final bow."

It's mind blowing to consider the vast difference between how the live shows were received in comparison to the album released at the time. Perhaps the moral of the story is that Rick and Roger were having a better time of it on stage rather than in the studio. Perhaps there would have been mileage in continuing as a live band. But when you consider that both Rick and Roger were innovators and constantly writing and creating new material, it is understandable as to why there needed to be a good rapport in the studio for the partnership to have been sustainable.

…*Famous Last Words*… was reviewed in *Record Mirror* in November 1982; "Perhaps they should call themselves Supercramp, since they've become so worn and dusty. Supertramp have become an ostrich with its head down in the sand, occasionally coming up for air. The stuffing's all but gone out of them and this is as wet as a dismal Friday."

Ouch! That's one of the toughest reviews by anyone's stretch of the imagination. For context, the magazine that this review featured in was, at the time, heavily enthusiastic about new wave and pop punk music. This interview is arguably symptomatic of what happened to many bands in the eighties who had earned their good reputation during the seventies; the media just didn't seem to have time for them anymore and the bands themselves were perhaps trying to work out where they could fit in amongst all this. Such phenomena would certainly stand to explain the change of musical direction in what was to be Supertramp's following album in 1985.

…*Famous Last Words*… was panned in a *Creem* review in April 1983; "This stuff is so bland already that the muzak folks are going to have their work cut out for them." Hodgson was quoted in *Jam* in September 1983; "I wasn't happy with our last album. From what I knew it could have been, it falls way short. I don't think that it is progression of anything that we have done in the past, and I don't think that it really hangs together. As far as running order goes, …*Famous Last Words*… is a prime example of wrong sequence. You have got 'Crazy', you've got 'Old Brown Shoe', which is a nice transition there, and then it should go somewhere else, but it doesn't. It kind of goes back to a track that probably should have opened the side, 'It's Raining Again'… There were only a couple of times on the European tour that when I saw the reaction of the people towards our music and how they obviously love it and the band, that I got a little sad knowing that this would be the last time that I would be performing with Supertramp. I am a little sad, but I am not sad for us. I just know that this is necessary to keep us, and especially myself, growing and producing music that is going to make other people happy. Perhaps Supertramp is too challenging for me now. It is really at a point now where for freshness and new growth, I need to find other musicians to work. With Supertramp I have gotten as much as I can from this collection of musicians. I still have a real deep love for them and them for myself, but I feel I need to work with other musicians for my creative growth."

In the same interview, Hodgson philosophised, "Each goal that you try to attain in life, it's the achieving of it that is the fun part. Once you have achieved this, hanging onto it for grim life, there is no happiness in that really unless it is still giving you something. If it's not, then you might as well go out and find a new mountain to climb, or a new goal to chase. I am very proud with what I have achieved with Supertramp, and I'm not trying to run away from it."

It's a shame that Roger's last album as a member of Supertramp is something that he wasn't pleased with. It would have been great had he have felt that he was leaving the band on a high in that regard. That said, even before …*Famous Last Words*… was recorded, there seems to be a sense that the writing was already on the wall.

John Helliwell
around the time
of the launch of
*...Famous Last
Words...* in late
1982.

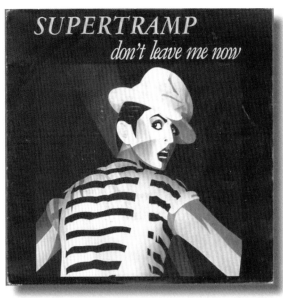

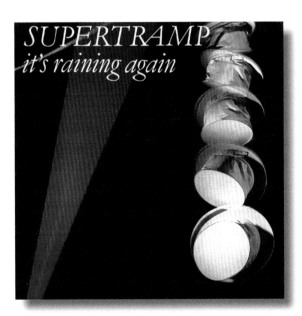

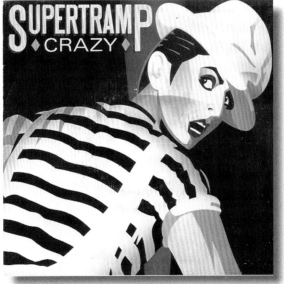

Chapter Nine:
Brother Where You Bound (1985)

**Brother Where You Bound
(1985)**

Rick Davies – keyboards,
lead and backing vocals
John Helliwell – saxophones
Dougie Thomson – bass
Bob Siebenberg – drums

David Gilmour – guitar
solos
Scott Gorham – guitar
Marty Walsh – guitar
Doug Wintz – trombone
Scott Page – flute
Cha Cha – backing vocals
Brian Banks – Synclavier
programming
Anthony Marinelli –
Synclavier programming
Gary Chang – Fairlight &
PPG programming

Side one
1. Cannonball
2. Still In Love
3. No Inbetween
4. Better Days

Side two
5. Brother Where You Bound
6. Ever Open Door

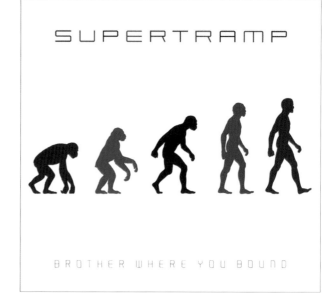

*B*rother Where You Bound was
Supertramp's eighth studio album
and the first to be made after Roger
Hodgson's departure. Supertramp were
now pretty much led by Rick Davies and
he was now in the driving seat in terms of
the songwriting and lead vocals. The album
was released in 1985 and was deliberately
a move away from the pop orientated music
of their previous two albums. *Brother Where
You Bound* got to number twenty in the UK
charts and number twenty one in the US
charts. The album included the top thirty
single, 'Cannonball'. The title track, was
a sixteen minute exposition on Cold War
themes augmented with guitar solos from
Pink Floyd's David Gilmour and rhythm guitar

played by Thin Lizzy's Scott Gorham. The track also includes readings from the George Orwell book, *Nineteen Eighty Four*. It's pretty inevitable that anything that references that book is likely to be very political in one way or another. The political themes were also apparent in the song, 'Cannonball' and 'Better Days', which featured extensive use of voiceovers from the four key players in the 1984 Presidential Campaign. Samples of spoken content from Geraldine Ferraro, Walter Mondale, George H.W. Bush and Ronald Reagan are mixed with an extended saxophone solo by John Helliwell.

A twenty-minute film of the album's title track was made by Rene Daalder and was used to promote the album. In an interview with *Billboard* in May 1985, Rick Davies was quoted as he discussed his reasoning as well as his concerns behind the album and its promotional film. I'm including the full transcription of the article because the interviewer's perspective also adds some interesting context to the points that Davies made;

"'It's hardly a commercial proposition', shrugs Davies, who allows that the film cost in the neighbourhood of half a million dollars. 'A twenty-minute film — there's no real place to show it.' But then again, he admits, 'a seventeen-minute track is near suicide' itself. Still, Supertramp has historically achieved sales success without relying on conventional marketing tactics. They were one of the premier 'faceless bands' of the last decade, but Davies is convinced that seventies low-profile techniques won't work in the eighties. 'We have to get better at video promotion', he conceded, 'before, we were recording and touring, and that was all we needed. We didn't need to push our faces, not that we were particularly pretty, anyway. Now, we have to put a little more of a front on things, to let people know we're around.' One hook for the new album is the appearance on the title track of ex-Pink Floyd guitarist David Gilmour. Although Hodgson has not been replaced in the group, Davies says he hopes Gilmour will tour with the band if his solo schedule allows. 'It was quite a Floydian track', says Davies of 'Brother Where You Bound', 'and we kept trying to get a guitar player to sound like Gilmour. Then somebody said, maybe David would come over and do it himself. And he did'."

Davies had already made a demo of the song, 'Brother Where You Bound' during the making of the band's previous album, ...*Famous Last Words*... but it didn't make it to that album because it was felt that it didn't fit with the overall theme. It could be considered that perhaps both Hodgson and Davies were given the creative space they needed to excel as individuals by parting ways. It is plausible that due to Roger Hodgson being honest with the rest of Supertramp about wanting to leave in 1983, there was not really much of a pause between Hodgson leaving and the Rick Davies led Supertramp beginning work on their next album. It was reported in *Gavin* in December 1984; "Despite the departure of guitarist Roger Hodgson, Supertramp is currently working on their next LP. Adding guitar parts to a few songs is David Gilmour of Pink Floyd."

Brother Where You Bound, and indeed Supertramp's new line-up, was reviewed in *Gavin* in May 1985; "With only Richard Davies remaining from the first edition of this band in 1970, you'd expect things to have changed. Actually, the transition hasn't been

SUPERTRAMP
'Brother Where You
Bound'
(A&M AMA 5014) ** ¾

HAVE YOU ever watched
Superstar Profile? It's a crummy
late-night TV import in which
some long-haired French bint
conducts incredibly boring
interviews with incredibly boring
long-haired 'superstars'. One such
programme featured some hairy
Scot pumping away at a Victorian
organ, wailing nasal nasties at a
distinctly unhealthy high pitch.
You guessed it – Supertramp.
    The hair is shorter now, the
men wear suits. To be fair,
'Brother Where You Bound' is far
more intelligent and *musical* than
90 per cent of US chart material –
but is that saying very much?
                                    ANDY HURT

that radical except 1) the late seventies saw them move from artistic self indulgence to a pop single sensibility and 2) they hit a creative slump with ...*Famous Last Words...* , their most recent album. But like the little tightrope walker on the cover of that famous album, they got back up and they're in fine form once again. They don't seem to miss the departed Roger Hodgson. Davies can handle the vocals. The mix is hot. The songs are crisp, albumy and more symmetrical than before. The artwork on the album cover is exceptional (fresh, clean and creative). Must be played to be heard. Super stuff. 'Cannonball' and 'Still In Love' lend themselves to the short and sweet formatics (sic) of most radio while they move heaven and earth with 'Brother Where You Bound' (aided by Pink Floyd's David Gilmour on guitar)."

I would suggest that the way the reviewer described Supertramp's line-up change was a bit of an overstatement. They made it sound like it was Rick Davies and a whole new cast. Nope. Not really. It was the line-up that most people consider to be that of classic Supertramp, just sans Roger Hodgson, plus a few others. I think what I'm getting at is that the reviewer's overstatement is a tad dramatic and therefore, somewhat misleading. Still though, a positive review.

With Davies at the helm of the band, more was done to promote the album than with their previous releases. To build public interest in *Brother Where You Bound*, it was premiered to members of the press travelling aboard a specially chartered trip from Paris to Venice on the Orient Express. On the trip, reporters were shown the full video for 'Brother Where You Bound'. This was certainly a change in promotion strategy from a band often renowned for being a low-profile group.

Cash Box reported in June 1985; "Venerable rock group Supertramp, minus the services of one-time member Roger Hodgson, are showing they can have success without their former band mate. Their latest album, *Brother Where You Bound* and single, 'Cannonball' are both doing very well on the charts this week. Supertramp is no stranger to the pop charts. The band's career has seen it top the charts time and time again. There was some question about Supertramp's future when it was announced last year that Roger Hodgson, responsible for half the band's songwriting and lead vocals, was splitting to pursue a solo career. *Brother Where You Bound*, the first Supertramp release featuring the new line-up with Rick Davies assuming all the writing and vocal duties, is an unqualified success. The album exhibits a solid national sales base."

In January 1986, it was announced in *Music & Media*; "Supertramp undertook a major European tour which started last week in France. The first Paris date was sold out in six hours and two extra ones were added. It is the first time that the band without Roger Hodgson embarks on such a huge tour. In January the band will play in France (eleven dates) and Spain (five dates). In February the band will visit France again (eight dates) as well as Holland, Belgium, Switzerland (one show each) and Germany (nine dates). From March 1st the band will play one gig in Zurich, two in Munich, one in Stuttgart and end at the Royal Albert Hall in London. Dates for Scandinavia and Italy are pending."

Meanwhile, Roger Hodgson had been focused on his solo career and by the time Supertramp released *Brother Where You Bound*, Hodgson's album had already been released and indeed with a strong sense of direction in terms of where he wanted to go with it. In October 1984, *Billboard* reported under the title of "Hodgson's New 'Storm' Hits Streets: Supertramp 'Divorce' Leads To Singer's Solo Debut."; "Los Angeles' Roger Hodgson announced in early 1983 that he was leaving Supertramp, of which he was a founding member, and that his solo album, *Sleeping With The Enemy*, would be released in the summer of 1983. Now, near the end of 1984, Hodgson's debut solo effort, entitled *In The Eye Of The Storm*, has finally hit the streets." Hodgson was quoted, "I scrapped the first attempt. I made that album under extreme duress and after listening to it I said 'No. That's not the kind of album I want to put out', so I shelved it… I'm ready to do battle. I've just done sixty-four interviews in four and a half days in Canada and after minimal promotion in America, I'm going on a major promotional tour of Europe… I think Supertramp had a reputation for quality and I think we made some great albums but the last two albums, the last four years, I think a lot of people lost interest in Supertramp. I certainly did… My studio is definitely going to pay for itself, even though I sunk a million dollars into it. I spent seven months in the studio on this album alone. When I went to mix it in New York it cost 125,000 dollars for only three weeks."

In the same article, it was stipulated that whilst Hodgson's studio had forty-eight track facilities that he had hopes to let friends use, there was no plan to use the space commercially. Whilst Roger was working on a 75,000 dollar video for the single, 'Had A Dream', his manager at the time, Doug Pringle, stipulated, "videos and film projects will play a large part in getting his image out there. Roger isn't a pop star. The focus of everything is directed to the music."

A somewhat contradictory statement there perhaps as in, surely music videos are predominantly the domain of pop stars? However, no matter how high profile someone was as a musician, the rise of MTV at the time was such that using video as a promotion tool for a single was perhaps becoming less and less optional and more of a necessity. All the same, life post Supertramp seemed to be treating Hodgson well in terms of him having the creative space to work how he wanted to on projects that he was enthusiastic about.

Billboard reviewed *In The Eye Of The Storm* in October 1984; "With Supertramp missing in action since his departure, singer, songwriter and multi-instrumentalist Hodgson captures much of the sweep and spirit of that band's melodic pop-rock style.

Largely self-contained instrumental work reaches for the same mix of layered vocals, massed keyboards and guitars and evocative production, especially on 'Had A Dream', which should capture fans of his old band at AOR and pop strongholds."

'Had A Dream' was reviewed in *Gavin* in October 1984; "Roger was obviously one of the whimsical voices of Supertramp. 'Had A Dream' will be the uptempo favourite off of Roger's new solo LP. Album radio is already embracing the single." *In The Eye Of The Storm* was reviewed in *Gavin* in October 1984; "If you already miss Supertramp then the first Roger Hodgson LP will fill the gap. Resplendent in the typical Supertrampish embellishments and excesses, *In The Eye Of The Storm* is heavy with song cycle theatrics and Hodgson's peculiar soprano stylising. Lyrics are loaded with I, Me and My intrapersonal visions. The music has the edge of rock and the orchestration of apocalyptic desperation. Just the sense of urgency and seriousness which didn't distinguish latter day Supertramp."

I might be wrong but the review reads like it was written by someone who was decidedly not a Supertramp fan. In such regard, it's difficult to comment objectively on such a review. *Music & Media* reviewed *In The Eye Of The Storm* in October 1984; "Written, arranged and produced by the former Supertramp frontman Roger Hodgson, the album continues in much the same vein as that band's successful melodic pop and rock style, a style that delivered more than thirty million albums worldwide. Tracks like 'Had A Dream', 'In Jeopardy' and 'Hooked On A Problem' all contain that unique combination of sparkling keyboards, strong catchy hooks and the typical voice of Hodgson, ingredients that make this album a noteworthy and commercial venture. The album comes in this week at number seventy in the European album charts (due to Germany, UK and Holland) and is about to break all over."

Hodgson was quoted in *Rolling Stone* in February 2012 as he explained what it had meant to him to give the Supertramp name to Rick Davies after he had left the band and had begun to pursue his solo career; "Back then I was Roger Hodgson with a lot of insecurities and unsure of myself, but I did have a passion for music, so it worked for me having a name, Supertramp, other than my name to just plow every ounce of my energy, passion and excitement into. I grew up on the Beatles and the Beatles profoundly changed my life, so, for me, they were the role models. I wanted Supertramp to affect other people like the Beatles affected me. I couldn't get behind Roger Hodgson being that name, I didn't have the kind of ego that wanted to be a solo artist back then. So I put all my passion into Supertramp and it was only really when I realised it was over and my heart was telling me I had to do something else and it was time to take a break from the music industry and learn how to be a parent that it dawned on me suddenly, I didn't have a name to continue a career. I was giving that name to Rick Davies. It was probably the most foolish business move I've ever done, but business was never my forte. My blessing and curse was that I was an artist first, I just had to follow my heart. So with Supertramp, two things were happening. It was very hard for me to function, even as an artist, towards the end, it was falling apart. It was frustrating because I wanted to continue putting out excellent music for people and I didn't feel like I could do it anymore through Supertramp. So that was happening at the same time two little babies were looking at me and I was saying, 'Oh my god, I've got to stop and learn how to be a parent', that was what my heart was telling me and I don't have any regrets today because I learned a lot from that, I stepped back from the music industry, I got a lot of things in perspective in my personal life."

Giving the Supertramp name over to Rick Davies has perhaps been something that Hodgson has had to address throughout his entire music career post Supertramp. In an interview with *Classic Rock Revisited* in February 2012, Hodgson was quoted on how him personally not being a household name came with a few barriers in terms of promoting his solo projects; "The name 'Roger Hodgson' isn't as well known as Supertramp. It was hard to get promoters to book the show. It is ironic because everyone knows my voice and, obviously, they know the songs because they have been listening to them for thirty to thirty-five years." In the same interview, Hodgson described how his agent decided to call his 2012 tour *The Breakfast In America Tour* "because it helps people connect the dots between my name and Supertramp."

Inevitably, fans and reviewers certainly seemed to be missing Roger Hodgson's presence from Supertramp, or at least commenting on it a lot. It's understandable that having made the band what it was in terms of its legacy, Hodgson was missed but equally, it could have easily been a source of frustration for the Davies led line-up of the band. Supertramp's live show at Universal Amphitheatre in California was reviewed in *Billboard* in December 1985; "When Supertramp co-founders Rick Davies and Roger Hodgson split, Davies said the stripped down version wouldn't go on the road to promote their *Brother Where You Bound* album because he had no intention of performing Hodgson's songs on stage. Davies changed his mind about not touring. If he had changed his mind about not performing Hodgson's songs, Supertramp's fine show of November 20th could have been upgraded to excellent. The venerable A&M act displayed admirable craftsmanship and professionalism in the one-hundred-minute set. It was the first of three nights at what is not a hometown venue for the group, and they really played up on the local connection. The stage was set clean and airy, the lights were stunning, and the use of historical footage on the widescreen backdrop added an absorbing narrative context. All of the crack sidemen could do vocals — an attribute that turned out to be vital, as only Davies from the remaining line-up can be said to sing. Versatile Scott Page played sax, flute, percussion and synthesiser. Mark Hart played synth and sang. Marty Walsh played rhythm guitar with a few stabs at lead and Carl Verheyen played lead guitar with a few stabs at rhythm. Each was generously afforded spotlight time and watching the interplay between the sidemen was a delight. They were so obviously delighted to be up there with such musicians' musicians. So why didn't the show draw more than one standing ovation? What shortcomings kept the audience off their feet the rest of the time? Maybe fans were hoping to hear some chat from bandleader Davies. Maybe they felt that not one, but two rock operas were a bit much for one show (during the fifteen-minute rendition of 'Brother Where You Bound', the lines for the restroom stretched across the lobby). But mostly, they missed the songs. If Davies was willing to cover Willie Dixon's 'I Just Wanna Make Love To You', why couldn't he cover Roger Hodgson's 'Logical Song' or 'Dreamer'? The best crowd reactions of the night, not surprisingly were for the Davies/Hodgson collaborations 'Bloody Well Right' and 'Goodbye Stranger'. Still, the single 'Cannonball' was rousing, the duelling saxes of Helliwell and Page were delicious and the pieces of director Rene Daalder's 'Brother' movie were fascinating. Davies apparently wants the 'new' Supertramp accepted on its own terms, and its own terms are acceptable enough. All the same, it would be nice if those rumours of a full band reunion were true."

Like many fans at the time, it seems that the reviewer was very much missing Hodgson's presence in Supertramp. The reasons for Davies not wanting to play Hodgson's songs upon his departure from the band is anyone's guess. It could be a diplomatic thing or indeed, it could be a technical thing, particularly when you consider the extent

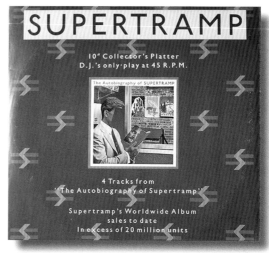

Rick Davies, May 1985
around the time of the launch of
Brother Where You Bound, the
first album without Roger, that
consisted entirely of
compositions by Rick.

John Helliwell and Scott Page at the Festival Hall, Frankfurt, 14th February 1986.

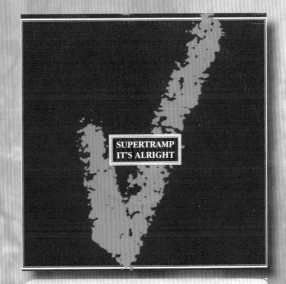

Supertramp Free as a bird

Chapter Ten:
Free As A Bird (1987)

Supertramp — Free as a bird

Supertramp's ninth studio album, *Free As A Bird*, marked another stylistic change in the direction of the band; they moved away from the progressive rock of the last album and moved more towards synthesised dance beats and rhythms. The *Free As A Bird* album was arguably symptomatic of what many bands who were successful in the seventies went through as they tried to find their feet in the eighties. The music world had changed so much by then, what with the rise of MTV and more music being created with computers and being more dance orientated. It is understandable as to why in such progress of perhaps trying to fit in commercially, Supertramp lost a lot of the essence of what they were originally about musically with the

Free As A Bird album. The single from the album, 'I'm Beggin' You' did okay as a single played in dance clubs (it reached number one in the US dance charts) but overall the album was sadly, a flop for the band; it failed to get into the top one hundred in America and it only got to number ninety-three in the UK.

As a result, it was the first of the band's albums to suffer such fate since *Indelibly Stamped* in 1971. Similarly, *Free As A Bird* was met with reasonable critical acclaim. It was reviewed in *Cash Box* in October 1987; "Britishers were big with keyboard flavoured, exotic rock arrangements in the seventies and early eighties. Now minus Roger Hodgson, Rick Davies takes over all writing and singing chores and provides plenty of light, appealing moments to carry the record. Highlights are 'It's Alright', 'Where I Stand' and 'I'm Beggin' You'."

Hmmm, it really does depend what yardstick a person chooses to use in terms of how to measure success though as in, *Free As A Bird* still managed to go gold in Canada, France, Spain and Switzerland. Canada seemed to remain consistently loyal to Supertramp throughout the band's career.

In terms of the band's line-up, Rick Davies was still leading it. *Free As A Bird* was the first of Supertramp's albums to feature Mark Hart on guitar and vocals. He would later go on to become a full member of the band. Supertramp disbanded after the *Free As A Bird* tour and would not reconvene until 1997, by which point it would be without Dougie Thomson on bass.

As part of the *Free As A Bird* tour, all of Hodgson's compositions were ditched from their set list. This was possibly also done as a means of further establishing Supertramp's new identity without Hodgson but in all fairness it could just have easily been an artistic decision. It's interesting that it happened but it's not my place to speculate on it, what with it being such a major and personal decision of those concerned.

Besides, when Supertramp did the Brazilian leg of their tour in 1988, a small number of Hodgson's songs were added back to the live set. As Helliwell was quoted in *Cash Box* in February 1988; "On stage, for the moment, we just do 'The Logical Song' and 'School'. We don't do a lot of Roger's songs because we can't do them justice. Some of them are so much his voice, like 'Dreamer' for example."

During this time, Roger Hodgson's career was ticking along nicely as he released his second solo album, *Hai Hai*, in September 1987. On the album, Hodgson was joined by some high-profile musicians; Jeff Porcaro (Toto), Nathan East (bassist for Phil Collins), Omar Hakim (drummer for Sting) and on synths, Robbie Buchanan.

In October 1987, *Billboard* announced; "Ex Supertamp keyboard player/guitarist/vocalist Roger Hodgson is back with 'You Make Me Love You', the first single from his just-released A&M solo album, *Hai Hai*. Meanwhile, look for a mid October release for the new Supertramp album, *Free As A Bird*."

Disappointingly though, the scope to do the amount of promotional work that he may have preferred to was taken away from Hodgson due to an injury. *Music & Media* declared in October 1987; "A get well soon message this week to Roger Hodgson, the former Supertramp vocalist who spent years getting his new solo LP *Hai Hai* together, then just two weeks before it is released, slipped and fell off a ladder, breaking both his wrists and suffering concussion. Hodgson will be in plaster for several weeks, sharply curtailing his promotional plans for the new album, which took some eighteen months to complete in his California studio. Hodgson's last album, *In The Eye Of The Storm*, sold more than one million copies worldwide."

That must have been devastating! Not only in terms of the injury itself but in terms of how the particular nature of said injury could have been a tremendous compromise on Hodgson's livelihood and indeed, his need to make music.

Still though, the reviews for *Hai Hai* and indeed the singles from it were generally very positive. *Hai Hai* was reviewed in *Billboard* in October 1987; "Distinctive voice of Supertramp goes solo with varied results. Lush tracks reminiscent of Hodgson's old band nestle side by side with more straightforward, hard-rocking material. A&M has uncannily released a Supertramp sound-alike, 'You Make Me Love You' as (an) initial single. 'Land Ho' could also push (the) album across with old fans."

Music & Media reviewed the album in October 1987; "Some contagious rocking pop gems, not much different, as 'Puppet Dance' proves, from his former work with Supertramp. However, 'London' and 'Desert Love' are wonderful." It also reviewed the single, 'You Make Me Love You'; "The singer's past with Supertramp shines through on this rich, evocative pop single, flavoured by his unmistakeable vocals."

'You Make Me Love You' was reviewed in *Cash Box* in October 1987; "Former Supertramp vocalist is flying solo. Familiar vocal style should capture listener attention almost immediately." *Billboard* gave a succinct review of 'You Make Me Love You' in October 1987; "Effective quick tempo pop from the former Supertramp member." *The Hard Report* reviewed 'You Make Me Love You' in September 1987 by quoting a number of radio station DJs; "Alan White — 'Roger's soprano pipes are instantly recognisable.' Rick Panneck — 'You can't deny that he has the signature Supertramp sound.' David Hall — 'This sounds like it could have been the next in the procession of hits that came from that classic album (*Breakfast In America*).' Jim Steel — 'His latest stands strongly on its own two feet. A fine piece to complement our playlist'."

The Hard Report stated in October 1987 of Hodgson's 'My Magazine'; "We had a feeling the joint release of Roger's solo and the Supertramp project had the makings of a super case of sibling rivalry — and now as both projects slide into the backup track stage, we've got to give Roger's deuce the decided advantage. He's got twelve stations now playing (the track)."

I think it's worth noting here that whilst *The Hard Report* framed things in a way that suggested that Hodgson and Supertramp were in competition with each other, I would suspect that both parties had graciously moved on and were simply focussing on their own projects. They were certainly both busy enough.

Luckily perhaps, Roger had already done a decent amount of promotional groundwork for *Hai Hai* before his injury. It was reported in *Billboard* in November 1987;

"Former Supertramp vocalist Roger Hodgson recently wrapped a video for 'London', a track from his new A&M album, *Hai Hai*. It's a conceptual piece in which Hodgson drives through the streets of Los Angeles reminiscing about his days in London. London sequences were shot by UK cinematographer, Douglas Milsome of *Full Metal Jacket* fame. Tony Vanden Ende directed. It was produced by Colleen McLean in Los Angeles and Roger Hunt in London for Vivid Productions."

In October 1987, an advert for 'You Make Me Love You' was featured in *Radio & Records*; "As keyboard player, guitarist and vocalist in Supertramp, Roger Hodgson helped create one of the most successful sounds ever. 'You Make Me Love You' picks up where he left off."

Notably, although it wasn't Roger's first solo project being advertised, it was still the case that the Supertramp name was possibly needed to promote him. Such was the extent to which individual members of the classic Supertramp didn't really become household names. Roger's contribution to Supertramp was clearly much loved and in such regard, it stands to reason that his previous membership with the band was referred to when it came to promoting him as a solo artist.

Besides, with or without Hodgson, the Davies led Supertramp was proactive in their marketing of *Free As A Bird*. It was reported in September 1987 in *Billboard*; "For Supertramp's *Free As A Bird*, due mid October, promotional frisbees should take flight any day. The album was produced by the band and mixed by Tom Lord-Alge to achieve a different Supertramp sound." Frisbees? Really? Yep, it happened. An image of one said frisbee was included next to the report.

Helliwell was quoted in *Cash Box* in February 1988 as he offered an insight into the *Free As A Bird* album; "It's the product of a jazzier influence being more predominant since Roger Hodgson left. I think it might have been Rick's writing with a drum machine that inspired some of the Latin feel. It's also the first album I've done with a horn section, and it gives a live feel… We had done a couple of light albums before making the last one with Roger, …*Famous Last Words*… which was another kind of light album. We just wanted to do something a little more serious. However, on this tour we felt that the 'Brother Where You Bound' piece would be too heavy so we won't be doing it live. The new album is a lot lighter again and that will be the vibe of the tour."

Chapter Eleven:
Some Things Never Change (1997)

Whilst studying for his A Levels, John Helliwell had planned to go on to the Royal College of Music. It didn't happen because by the age of eighteen he had secured a job as a computer programmer in Birmingham working for ICL, Britain's biggest computer firm at the time. It was when things slowed down with Supertramp that Helliwell enrolled to study at the Royal Northern College of Music in Manchester.

By the time of the *Some Things Never Change* album, although Helliwell was well into his degree course, he left in order to do the tour for that album. Although as the oldest student on his course, John dropped his degree, he still associates with the institution and in the summer of 2019, he played a concert there as a professional show. In 1996, Helliwell played on Roger Hodgson's third solo album, *Rites Of Passage*, a live album featuring the music from a short tour (Hodgson released his fourth solo album, *Open The Door* in 2000 and *Classics Live* in 2010).

In 1993 there was hope that Rick Davies and Roger Hodgson may begin working together again. On 14th April at the Beverly Hills Hilton, a special dinner was held in honour of Jerry Moss, co-founder of A&M records. It was reported in *Radio & Records* in April 1993; "A&M Chairman Jerry Moss was honoured at Cities In Schools' first LA fundraiser, which raised more than 1.2 million dollars. The organisation announced that the first Jerry Moss Music Resource Centre will be established in California to support public school students who don't have access to such non-academic courses as music classes. On hand for the event were CIS founder Bill Milliken, Supertramp members Roger Hodgson and Rick Davies, and Moss."

At the event, Hodgson, Davies and Helliwell performed 'The Logical Song' and 'Goodbye Stranger'. This seemed to get the ball rolling for Davies and Hodgson and they began working together again whereby they recorded demos for two new songs, 'You Win, I Lose' and 'And The Light'. It was apparently management related disagreements that resulted in the pair parting ways once again. Soon after, the two songs would appear on Supertramp's 1997 album, *Some Things Never Change*, sans Hodgson of course. In 1996 Davies re-formed Supertramp with Helliwell, Siebenberg and guitarist/vocalist Mark Hart, who was new to the official line-up but had substantially contributed to the *Free As A Bird* album and its supporting tour.

This reunion resulted in the album, *Some Things Never Change*. It was released in March 1997 and it was more in line with the earlier Supertramp sound that people were familiar with. The album got to number seventy-four in the UK charts and the single, 'You Win, I Lose' was given plentiful radio play in Canada. A unique feature of the *Some Things Never Change* album was in how the recording process for it was more cohesive whereby all band members worked together in the studio at the same time.

The tour for the album in summer 1997 resulted in the release of their live album in 1999, *It Was The Best Of Times*. It was reported in *Gavin* in February 1998; "Supertramp re-grouped without Roger Hodgson last year for a brief tour and has just released an album with three singles. Now it appears Hodgson will release his own new music and also hopes to tour this spring."

In September 1996, *Music & Media* had announced; "Work has started on a new album due out in 1997 to be released on Chrysalis in the UK and on EMI in the rest of the world." It also stated that it was not clear as to whether or not Roger Hodgson would be involved in the project. I suppose from the media's point of view, it is possible that there were still hopes of the classic line-up reforming, even though in reality, it was likely the case that the band themselves knew that this wasn't going to be.

It is likely that touring may have been necessary in the name of promotion for both Supertramp and Roger Hodgson. In *Music & Media* in March 1997, it was announced that *Some Things Never Change* was due for release on the 24th of the month on EMI. Reasonably, the reporter considered, "A decade after their last studio album and after a decade which has seen the rise of music styles from techno to Britpop, the challenge for Supertramp is to prove that their well crafted melodic pop-rock is still fit for the end of the century."

In the same article, Rick Davies was quoted from what he had said at a recent promotional press conference that had been held in Paris; "Supertramp is not a band from the nineteen seventies or the nineteen eighties. Such would be the case if we didn't exist anymore. Today, we are simply Supertramp. We are made to last."

The article stipulated that a fifty date European tour that was due to begin in Sweden on 27th April was selling well to the point that many gig dates had already sold out and that the single, 'You Win, I Lose' was doing well on European radio. However, some radio stations just weren't willing to embrace Supertramp or their new music.

In the article, the programme director (Laurent Bouneau) for French network Skyrock was quoted; "One song out of two we play on Skyrock is rap and the rest is dance, R&B and groovy stuff. We have a tight format and have almost completely dropped playing big names from the seventies or the eighties like Sting or Phil Collins. This is not a judgement on the quality of their music, it simply doesn't match our format." In other words, no matter what music Supertramp happened to be making in 1997, the very fact that they were Supertramp was enough to be a barrier to getting heard on some stations. The fickle nature of the music industry!

In 2001, Roger Hodgson played with Ringo Starr in the All Starr Band. Ringo was quoted in *Billboard* in May 2001 in a promotional interview for the upcoming tour. Starr said of working with Roger Hodgson (as well as Howard Jones, Sheila E., Mott The Hoople's Ian Hunter and Greg Lake); "I love to play with people who shine. That's what it's always been about for me. We're all playing together."

Hodgson was quoted in *Record Mirror* in March 1975; "When I was a kid it was the Beatles — full stop, but I never saw them live. I didn't see myself going to a concert full of screaming kids and the only opportunity was to see them in a situation like that." So Roger didn't get to see the Beatles play live but he did get to play on stage with Ringo Starr. Life has some of the strangest twists and turns!

142

Rick Davies performing in Vienna for the German TV show *Wetten, dass..?*, 22nd March 1997.

Chapter Twelve:
Slow Motion (2002)

Slow Motion (2002)

Rick Davies – keyboards,
harmonica, lead and
backing vocals
Mark Hart – guitars,
keyboards, lead and
backing vocals
John Helliwell – saxophone,
woodwind
Cliff Hugo – bass
Bob Siebenberg – drums
Lee Thornburg – horns,
backing vocals
Carl Verheyen – guitars
Jesse Siebenberg – drums,
backing vocals

1. Slow Motion
2. Little By Little
3. Broken Hearted
4. Over You
5. Tenth Avenue Breakdown
6. A Sting In The Tail
7. Bee In Your Bonnet
8. Goldrush
9. Dead Man's Blues

After a three-year break, Supertramp reunited in 2002 to make another album, it was released in the April of that year. The *One More For The Road* tour immediately followed. Compared to Supertramp's previous albums, *Slow Motion* was pretty much a small-scale project; In North America it was initially only available via mail order from the band's website. It was released on their own label. One song on the album, 'Goldrush', was actually written in the 1970's by the very first line-up and it was used as an opening number in their live sets prior to *Crime Of The Century* taking off. However, when the band had tried previously to record the song in the studio, they had never been happy enough with it to use it at that time. As with other Supertramp tours sans Roger Hodgson, the band used songs from the Hodgson era in their 2002 live set.

After the *One More For The Road* tour, Supertramp were inactive again. As ever, the rumour mill in the media would sometimes bring up the subject of a possible reunion between Davies and Hodgson but the evidence pretty much speaks for itself as in, it didn't happen.

Hodgson has been very much dedicated to his solo career since leaving the band. In July 2007 he performed at the *Concert For Diana* that was held in London at Wembley Stadium to celebrated Princess Diana's life. Hodgson performed 'Dreamer', 'The Logical Song', 'Breakfast In America' and 'Give A Little Bit'. As was reported in *Billboard* in May 2007, "Artists Added To Diana Concert Bill… Nelly Furtado, P. Diddy, Tom Jones, Will Young and Supertramp frontman Roger Hodgson have been added to the list of performers for the *Concert For Diana*, to be held July 1st at London's new Wembley Stadium. The concert was conceived by Prince Harry as a celebration of their mother Diana, who died in a Paris car crash in 1997."

Hodgson expressed his admiration for Princess Diana as he was quoted in *Goldmine* in November 2007; "I was delighted to be invited by the princes, because I just really thought the world of Princess Diana. I thought she was handed a very, very difficult role and handled herself very well, and turned her fame into what now a lot of performers are, using for philanthropic matters. When you're famous, what can you do with it? You can't… there's a limit to how much it can feed your ego. At some point, the ones who are smart, the Angelina Jolies, the Brad Pitts, the Princess Dianas, they realise okay yeah, I can use all the cameras… to bring all the cameras to something that's more important than just me. Which is all the causes in the world that really need attention, so I really admire what she did with her life. And I never got to play for her in person when she was alive, so I was very happy to have that desire fulfilled in a way by honouring her on her tenth anniversary."

Hodgson was quoted in *Goldmine* in November 2007 as he described his experience of the concert; "When I watch the Princess Di performance, it's really just a man and his music, naked out there, just singing, and enjoying it. And believe me, it was not the easiest situation going on in front of 80,000 people with a voice that was not working particularly well that day and pulling it off. And you know, I literally pulled it off with just enjoying myself, and I got the place on its feet and they were singing along, doing 'Give A Little Bit' with me, and it went off great, but there's something with all the paraphernalia of all the productions and all the stuff that can get away, really, for me, it starts with heart to heart. It's my heart to the audience's heart, and everything else gets in the way of that. It doesn't have to. It can embellish it. But the beauty of what I'm doing is, literally, it's a man and his music and either you like it or you don't."

On 21st April 2010, it was announced that Supertramp would perform thirty-five concerts later that year in Europe. The tour was titled *70-10* to commemorate the 40th anniversary of the band's first release. During such time, Roger Hodgson was fully committed to a solo tour covering Australia, New Zealand, South America, Europe, Canada and the US. The commitment was such that Hodgson reuniting with Supertramp would not have been possible at that time regardless of how different parties concerned may have felt about the matter.

Again, there are rumours about who said what and why etc etc moan, moan, but as ever, I don't feel that it is appropriate to speculate on them here because 1) it was completely between Hodgson, Davies and their managements and 2) everyone knows what happened; there was no reunion and there is yet to be one… if any! Don't hate me readers but the decision for Davies and Hodgson not to reunite does seem logical as in, if the musical and personal harmony just isn't there, what would be the point? It would surely make for a very strained project. On the nostalgia front, there are a lot of classic Supertramp albums to take for a spin.

It seems that Roger is happy to remain as a solo artist rather than seek to make a Supertramp reunion happen. As he was quoted in *Rolling Stone* in February 2012, "One of the reasons I'm a solo artist really is because I can control what happens between me and the audience. To me, it's a very magical, chemical, energetic connection that happens on stage every night I can control. And I can't control that in a band situation; it becomes something else. And I think Supertramp, for me, was a very good combination of musicians in the golden years. And Rick and I, that was a very interesting yin and yang polarity that really made for an interesting dynamic and often does. But that was at least thirty years ago now. Rick and I did talk, but it's hard to reinvent what people want to see, it wouldn't be real. It would be more imaginary, but I'm aware that there's a real desire for a lot of fans around the world to want to see it happen. The last thing that happened was I did put out an offer when Rick went out as Supertramp to maybe join him for a few shows. And there was a negative answer, I got rebuffed, so I think that was the last opportunity really. And to tell you the truth, I'm more interested in just being true to myself and giving people something I can stand behind and be sincere about. I'd have to compromise that if it was a whole Supertramp hoopla thing. As magic as that might be, I can understand why other bands don't do that."

To his credit, Hodgson seems to have been consistent in his stance on not being keen to do a Supertramp reunion. He was quoted in the *St Louis Post Dispatch* in May 1998; "I get asked everyday 'do you think you might ever get back together (with Davies) again' but you know, it's really hard to go back and recapture old magic. Everyone would like to see the old magic there in some shape or form but it's very hard to go back. I kind of liken it to going back to an ex-wife and expecting there to be sparks and magic there again. You can't do it. That's not to say that there wouldn't be something for old time's sake, or maybe we'll be brought together for another reason just for fun."

Supertramp went inactive again between 2011 and 2015. Meanwhile, in 2012, Hodgson began his global *Breakfast In America Tour*. With dates on and off during such period, the tour eventually concluded in December in Nova Scotia. As was reported in February 2012 in *Rolling Stone*; "By 1979, Supertramp was one of the biggest rock bands in the world, with *Breakfast In America* spending fifteen weeks at number one on the US album charts. Four years later, Roger Hodgson left the band he helped make famous. Now, after twenty-nine years, a smiling Hodgson is kicking off his first US band tour since '83 at Pechanga Casino & Resort in Temecula, California. Yes, it's a world away from the stardom he would totally turn his back on when he left music in '87 to concentrate on being a parent. But to the adoring fans who rise to their feet as Hodgson and his four-piece backing band take the stage just after 8:00 with the FM radio staple 'Take The Long Way Home', it might as well be 1979 all over again."

In the same article, Hodgson was quoted, "Everyone pretty much knows my voice, they know my songs, but they don't know my name. And I didn't think about that when I left Supertramp. Supertramp was a kind of faceless band. Supertramp was my baby in a way and I was quite happy to be invisible in it because I put fourteen years of my life in there and that's what I believed in, never thought I'd leave it. It was a surprise for me in a way when suddenly my heart was telling me that it's over and I need to stop and take care of my family and learn how to be a father."

The vast legacy of Supertramp's popular songs is such that when touring in 2012, Hodgson was tasked with needing to strike a balance between wanting to showcase his new material whilst giving audiences the much loved classic material. Not the worst complaint for a musician to have, I'm sure. But still, it is certainly testament to Supertramp's legacy and what that means for Roger Hodgson as a solo artist.

He was quoted in *Classic Rock Revisited* in February 2012; "My biggest problem is what songs not to play in my show. Undoubtedly, someone will write in and say, 'Why didn't you play this song?' The trouble with having so many songs that people have such a relationship with is that it makes it hard to tell them that they are going to have to listen to thirty minutes of new music. As great as the new songs are, for me as an artist, I want to give people the deepest experience that I can. If that means playing the songs that people have the deepest relationship with and maybe throwing in a few new ones, then I will do that. I won't say they have to listen to thirty minutes of new songs. I do have a lot of new songs and they are wonderful songs and I will have to figure out a way to share them with people at some point. For now, I try to share maybe one or two of them during the show and introduce them that way."

In the same interview, he continued, "The bottom line is that there is an incredible love for Supertramp. When the people think of Supertramp they think of the music that was created, so much of which were my songs. If people want to hear that again, they do have another opportunity in my shows. People tell me all the time that it felt like a Supertramp show to them. I think that is because I was so much the heart and soul of Supertramp and these songs were such a huge part of it."

It comes across that Hodgson has always been more about the music than playing the fame game. He was quoted in *Rolling Stone* in February 2012 as he expressed what coming back to touring meant to him after having had some time out from the industry; "I'm coming back now a lot older, a lot wiser, and I feel with a lot more to give. And ironically with a lot of the same songs that haven't aged. It's funny, I sing these songs on stage, this is the first time I've sung them really for three months, and it's like, 'Wow, these songs are great.' It took a long while (to get to this point). Really I'm Roger Hodgson now not because I have a huge desire to have a huge career and be a huge name. I like being just under the radar, famous enough to do shows like this, have an intimate connection with an audience, play my songs and connect with people in a real kind of pure way. I don't want to dive into the whole star machine. When you come and see the show, it's a man and his music… It's hard not to compromise. Sometimes you piss away a career if you don't compromise, but at least you can sleep good at night as an artist. And, to me, with the music industry going more and more into star making and fashion, it's been trivialised. I grew up on the Beatles and there was a lot of depth to them, they were the most progressive band ever. They broke the doors down and it feels like there aren't that many artists doing that now. I'm certainly not breaking the doors down, but I'm trying to give something that's real and genuine. This is my music and if I can make you feel wonderful for two hours and go home with a smile on your face, then come and see the show."

Bob Siebenberg was quoted in *Modern Drummer* in December 2014; "Being on the stage with Supertramp back then was a totally focused affair. I was always listening and inside the tune. I would start playing along in my head as my spot approached, and my body would start to move as if I was already playing, and bang. So I was totally in before I actually started. It's a great band to play in. The band was always very, very focused on the music."

It's plausible that Hodgson is happy to have the control over his music — facilitated by him being a solo artist who is not aiming for superstardom. As he was quoted in *Classic Rock Revisited* in February 2012; "I played Wembley Stadium with 60,000 people, alone, four or five years ago. I wouldn't want to do that as a steady diet, believe me. To tell you the truth, for me, performing, now, is about connecting and having people feel the emotions that I am putting into the songs. That can get lost in a big stadium where the sound is reverberating around; you lose all the nuances. I'm just a dot on the stage for most people. The smaller places sound much better. People pay a lot of money to come see me and not only does it sound better, they can see me, they can feel me and they can connect with me and I can connect with them. The feeling we can generate over two hours is much more powerful than in a stadium. A stadium is a much different experience. I've done that extensively with Supertramp and it has its own type of thrill. I prefer the kind of connection that I can make with audiences in a two to three thousand seater."

It seems to be the case that Roger has predominantly been more about the music itself rather than thinking of it in commercial terms. As he was quoted in *The San Diego Union Tribune* in February 2011; "For me, music was where I went to express my longing to know God, to know true love, my longing to feel truly at home inside myself. I put this inner quest into my songs and I believe, because they came from such a deep place, this is one of the reasons they have had such an enduring quality. They touch that place in everyone who is searching for true happiness, belonging, for God — whatever you want to call it. So yes, most of my songs have a spiritual theme in them — when I write music, I am always alone and it's very much an inner communion for me. It's not generally known that I never wrote with the band, and the band didn't share many of the spiritual beliefs that I wrote about — so all my songs — new and old — are all very personal expressions from me."

For Hodgson, the creativity and the fulfilment he seems to get from making music has perhaps been a key driver throughout his career. I appreciate that could be quite a strong assumption to make but there is much consistency in how Hodgson speaks of such motives. He was quoted in September 2010 in *The Huffington Post*; "The songs I contributed to Supertramp came from a very pure place in my soul. They were not contrived for any mere commercial purpose — simply to write 'hit' songs. Without even being fully aware of it, I created these songs to explore my very private longing for love and that sense of a true home, a place of real connection inside our heart. Though even I did not fully understand it at first, I now know that these songs were vehicles for me to try and figure out answers to the fundamental questions of life. That's why I never get tired of singing my songs. The songs that I have written are, in a sense, the purest and deepest expression of who I am. I believe that's why songs like 'Dreamer', 'Give A Little Bit', 'Take The Long Way Home' and 'The Logical Song' continue to be meaningful to me, and to so many other people around the world."

The Davies led Supertramp announced a 2015 European tour entitled *Supertramp Forever*. It was due to begin in Portugal on 3rd November and finish on 11th December in Amsterdam. However, on 4th August 2015, the band announced that the tour would not be possible due to health issues affecting Rick Davies; he had been diagnosed with multiple myeloma that required treatment.

König-Pilsener-Arena,
Oberhausen, Germany,
30th May 2002.

Gerry Weber Stadion,
Halle, Germany,
2nd September 2010

dpa picture alliance / Alamy Stock Photo

Chapter Thirteen:
A Continuing Legacy

I would suggest that a lot of the charm about Supertramp, aside from their fantastic music, is that the classic line-up of the band consisted of five very different musicians with a range of talents and a diversity across many different musical genres.

John Helliwell was quoted in *Sounds* in May 1976; "It's all subconscious, we don't try and do anything in a particular style. We're just five diverse influences playing music and if you listen you can really hear quite a bit. All we really want to do is to get across to as many people as possible."

The band seemed to be very much a team effort in terms of how everyone brought something interesting and worthwhile to the table; where some excelled, others were perhaps less interested but that didn't really seem to matter when you consider that their musical output overall was such a collective effort.

For instance, Rick Davies was quoted in *Melody Maker* in June 1979 as he described his lack of interest in the production side of things; "There's no real powerhouse musician in the band. Because of that, I think that we need to be fussy in the production… (Roger Hodgson is) welcome to it. If I ever did a solo album, I'd just get the best producer I could think of and leave it to him. I skived a lot when we did *Breakfast In America*. It just gets beyond being any fun at all. You'll walk in and they're playing a certain section and five hours later they're still on it, but I'm certainly grateful for the results. I would just add to the confusion if I hung about."

Fair enough. Davies did more than enough as a writer and musician. Play to your strengths and all that. In the same piece, Davies was quoted as having said that the eight months it took to record *Breakfast In America* was "a ridiculous amount of time really."

With regards to production, Roger Hodgson was quoted in the same article; "We have a reputation now for high quality so we can't release bad sound quality. If you left me to my own devices I'd go home with my eight track stereo recorder and probably put an album out on that. The albums I like aren't of very high recording quality. If you listen to all the Beatles' stuff, it's terrible, it was recorded abominably but because the vibe in it is so nice, you don't even think about it." It comes across that Hodgson and Davies were unified in their appreciation of having a good producer.

It is fascinating to think that the differences between the members of Supertramp was perhaps a blessing as much as it was a curse, in the sense that, whilst their differences as individuals made for amazing musical collaboration, I am convinced that there were business decisions made that suited different people to various extents (if at all!).

A prime example here would be the move to America and how each of them

Philharmonic Hall, Liverpool,
29th May 2011.

© Ian Fairbrother/Alamy Stock Photos

Canada has always been a great market for Supertramp. Rick is giving his all here at Molson Amphitheatre, Toronto, Canada, 12th June 2011.

felt about it. I'm taking the wildest of guesses but with Bob Siebenberg already being from America in the first place, moving back there may not have been the ingredient for homesickness that it could have been for the others. As I say though, that's literally just me taking a guess at things. That aside, understandably, everyone seemed to have a different feeling about the move to America.

John Helliwell was quoted in *Record Mirror* in April 1977; "There's a lot of freeways here, terrific wide roads. The trouble is, many people are half asleep when they're driving along and if you nip in and out between the cars you're defying death. And you should see it when it's wet. They're just not used to it — cars all over the place. It's a strange place. It takes a bit of getting used to, I can tell you. LA is just a big smoggy sprawl. It's okay down on the beach though. You don't get the smog there for some reason. Must be a wind off the basin… You can't get a decent pint here. I shall be glad to taste some decent beer when we come back (to the UK) in the summer… There's plenty of good jazz over here. More choice than in London anyway. I saw Weather Report recently. They were fantastic… Roger Hodgson is a spiritual seeker and he's found a circle of friends here and has been very productive as a song writer as a result… I don't know where we'll end up. I don't think I want to live in LA always. I want to live somewhere green."

I would advocate that Helliwell probably wasn't being disparaging of America. Many people would be tripped out at moving to a completely different country, I would imagine. Besides, there was certainly a plan behind the move. As Helliwell continued, "We came over here to consolidate our position in the States. We wanted to really attack the places we weren't known. There are still some cities we have to make an impression on. It's true that we had to do it at the expense of our own country but we're looking forward to playing back there when our world tour brings us to Britain at the end of the summer. I miss the place."

It was certainly happening all at once. Helliwell added; "We're a week and a half into the tour and having to curtail gigs due to illness. We had to cut one gig short and cancel another, as Roger's voice gave way. We've all had colds, even though the weather's quite good. We've been playing with Gallagher and Lyle, and now Procol Harum. We're touring with John Miles next. I want to have a look at Harum — suss them out before we go out there and play. Their drummer has always been one of my heroes… I'd like to do an album of my own one day. But that won't be for a long time yet. We've got too much work on at present over here. America is such a big place to break. It took Peter Frampton two years to break here." Incidentally, the title of this article was that of, "Homesick Tramp"!

It comes across that Hodgson was perhaps the happiest of the four British members of Supertramp to have moved to America. Roger was quoted in *Melody Maker* in June 1979; "I started getting into yoga and spiritual things in England, but you could say it found fertile soil in California. Yoga is considered weird in England but in California it's not. It's an everyday word that people have a lot of respect for and it's what a lot of people are into. The same as being vegetarian. In England you're a weirdie. So there's that and the climate. In California, you feel that you want to be healthy, because you feel good. In England, unfortunately, you almost live your life in a raincoat. That was my biggest reason for living in California."

Rick Davies might not have been as pleased about the move though. He was quoted in the same feature; "As we live in LA, it's very hard to say whether or not we've settled down in America. I don't think that's a place where anybody wants to settle down, not even Americans. It's a kind of limbo place. It's a love-hate thing with me. I tend to breathe a sigh of relief when I get back there (the UK). The TV over here (USA) is horrible."

Again though, it is the differences between Rick and Roger that probably made them the strong partnership that they were. Even though they wrote the songs separately, what they produced together was certainly a big deal both musically and commercially in the grand scheme of things. Roger cited the Beatles as a strong influence in a number of interviews and his approach to music also comes across as being very philosophical. He was quoted in *Melody Maker* in June 1979; "Rock 'n' roll is just touching upon what's possible with music. I really think of rock 'n' roll as being very primitive. We haven't even begun to explore. The power of music has been forgotten. The ancients knew it and we're rediscovering it very slowly. Music has the power to heal, to hypnotise, to make people totally sad, happy, joyous. I'd like to find out how to do all those things."

That's not to say though that Rick Davies wasn't philosophical in his approach to music, it may just be the case that Roger Hodgson has been more outspoken on such front. Of course, Rick's musical background and inspirations were very different to Roger's. Rick was quoted in April 1975 in *Beat Instrumental* as he offered a detailed insight into his musical influences; "I am influenced by standards rather than actual influences. I'm very conscious of whether a number is up to so-and-so's standard, or whether it's naive or what. As far as lyrics go it's gotta be Dylan, I'm not saying I try to write like Dylan but when you hear people like that you can't really get too cocky about writing lyrics."

In the same feature, Davies listed Steve Winwood and Stevie Wonder as good musicians and that when he got the opportunity, he liked to listen to "funky jazz things like Horace Silver, sixties jazz and Blue Note records". He continued, "I really admire that music because it's a rare combination of technique and feel. In the rock field you tend to get too much technique and the feel gets lost, or you get a very kind of primitive heavy thing, which is lacking in technique, whereas those albums I mentioned just hit both nails on the head… When I see an album, I like an album to be an album which is a complete thing, not a concept in that it's got to be a story or a rock opera or anything, but it's gotta have a mood all the way through, I think that's right. That's why I don't play these 'Best Of' albums because you're getting a lot of the different times of people. Singles are okay but we don't aim any of our numbers at singles."

It was reported in the same article that Rick found it to be the case that lyrical ideas came to him at any time but with regards to musical ones, as he was quoted, "I find out on stage by jamming." He stipulated that whilst he and Roger wrote separately, they would then "turn the songs round among ourselves." With his influences being imbedded in jazz, it makes absolute sense that Davies grew his musical ideas out of jamming.

Of course, Rick and Roger had quite a number of things in common in their approach to music; they were both predominantly self taught on piano and were both incredibly strong musicians on a number of instruments. It seems that this passion and drive was probably very effective when it came to Supertramp. It is possible that being self taught at piano went in Rick Davies' favour from a creative perspective. He was quoted in *Beat Instrumental* in April 1975; "I'm still really trying to play the piano in a lot of ways. My approach to the piano is still very primitive even now. I'm not saying it's wrong, I still get a great buzz out of playing, but you're frightened to decide whether to try to learn more and run the risk of losing the freshness of discovering new things which come when you're writing and you discover new chords and things that help the writing, so you're frightened that if you get too knowledgeable it might stifle something."

There is no denying that Rick and Roger's writing partnership resulted in some phenomenal and much-loved material being made. However, their differences were certainly there when it came to the specifics of their writing rapport. That is something that may explain why they wrote their songs separately before collaborating together when it came to recording them. There's no definitive answer on that one so I certainly don't wish to fuel any rumours in such regard.

What is evident though is that within the writing partnership, Rick and Roger were very much two individuals. Roger was quoted in *Melody Maker* in June 1979 regarding the title track of *Breakfast In America*; "If Rick had his way, it wouldn't have been on this album either. He never liked the lyric to 'Breakfast In America' — it's so trite — 'Take a look at my girlfriend', he's much more into crafting a song. He would have been happier if I'd changed the lyric to either something funnier or more relevant. I tried, but it didn't work out, so I was stuck with the original."

In the same feature, Rick agreed that he wasn't keen on 'Breakfast In America' (both the song and as a title for the album) but that he came round to Roger's way of thinking when he considered that in context, the album was very much a pop orientated album. Rick was quoted; "That title almost allows for pop songs. The actual song, 'Breakfast In America', doesn't seem to mean much. Neither do 'Oh Darling' or 'Goodbye Stranger' so I saw a shape and it fitted. The pop side has always been a part of the group's character. Maybe it's been swamped a bit by the Genesis comparison but it's always been there. In a way, it's easier to write minor key opuses than a really good catchy pop song. That's not easy at all. Roger has a stack of them a mile high, you know… I probably get more annoyed about the words than anybody else. I think 'The Logical Song' is nice. I like 'Casual Conversations' but I think, for example, that 'Goodbye Stranger' and 'Oh Darling' could go a bit deeper than they do. I feel a lack of somebody pushing me in the lyrical area. In all the other areas — singing, playing, arranging — there's always somebody on top of you, drawing out the best."

In the June 1979 *Melody Maker* feature, the journalist certainly picked up on (or at least portrayed) Davies and Hodgson as an odd couple; "Roger Hodgson floats around like the Holy Ghost. Dressed in white, an angelic picture, he could easily pass for Robert Powell's understudy in *Jesus Of Nazareth*. He is Rick Davies' diametric opposite, more willing to share his feelings, less morose while engaged in his search for The Light. While Davies looks as if he's carrying the worries of the world on his shoulders. Hodgson's carefree outlook creates a striking contrast. Hodgson's unorthodox approach to touring is one reason why he isn't as hung up as his counterpart. While the rest of the band flit around America by jet, Hodgson and his wife and eight-week-old baby girl follow them in his motorhome."

Hodgson was quoted; "One of the reasons touring is so wearing is that there's no grounding influence. The great thing about a motorhome is that you can keep your own space. A motorhome is a hotel room on wheels, but at least it's your own hotel room."

Even in 1977, even before *Breakfast In America*, it seems that the seeds of disagreement had, at least to an extent, been sown. Roger was quoted in *New Musical Express* in August 1977; "I think we've got to talk about what we want to do in the future. Our writing styles are such that two things have to happen. Solo albums have to be made and there's got to be a Supertramp direction established. If those two things happen, it should really work out great. It's just that we haven't established what the Supertramp direction is going to be. There's going to be a different direction because the area where all five of us gel best has been evident on home tapes. On those we've been blowing and interacting with each other and not just going through, well they're not exercises, but it's a pretty disciplined set of songs we do on stage at the moment. Our audience loves it, but maybe we should be courageous and get slagged to hell — go the way the strength of the band lies, which is when we're all communicating with each other musically. We're all very aware of what hasn't been done so far and all the music that's still lying around. Something will come up. The vibe in the band has never been better, and if it does fall apart then it will happen naturally rather than nastily, but I can't see any reason why it should… No matter how much we try and establish a direction for the band, and even for the world, everything happens naturally at its own pace and in its own time. The band might fold at the end of this tour. We might still be together in five or six year's time… Shit! I've been with Rick eight years now, as long as we keep learning and getting something from it, that's all that really matters." Succinctly, in the same interview, Rick was quoted; "The group's not going to last forever."

For every person who has been touched or influenced by the music of Supertramp (Roger was quoted in *Melody Maker* in November 1975; "We got a letter from someone saying that 'Dreamer' is their eighteen month old kid's favourite record. Somehow I don't think that's typical"), it is worthwhile to consider some of their musical influences.

In *Piano News* in January 2011, Hodgson was quoted; "One of my biggest influences was Claude Debussy. His music touched me in a very deep way because it was so different from the classical music I knew; more free, more colourful and the sound more beautiful. In particular I remember the piano pieces, 'The Girl With The Flaxen Hair' and 'Clair De Lune'. That one I found so beautiful it could have made me cry. The rolling melody, the lucent tunes. The thing that fascinated me most about Debussy was the fact that there is no such thing as an exact reprise. It's like a journey into the unknown and thus totally different from a pop song with the well-known sequence of verse-chorus-verse-chorus. As far as Debussy is concerned, there's always progress in his music and in the end it will return home safely. In my genre, rock and pop, there are lots of reprises and there are often very formulaic structures. With many of my songs, I have attempted to avoid just that. There is always progress — just like with Debussy."

In the same interview, Hodgson mentioned his appreciation for *The Planets* by Gustav Holst as well as the Beatles; "Like so many others I have grown up to their music and I virtually soaked them in. The Beatles' influence on my artistic development is immense! Lennon was a huge role model in many ways. I was most impressed by the artist who was able to express his most inner feelings. And then there are his piano pieces like 'Imagine' or 'Across The Universe', which are simply great. I wish I'd written them. Lennon was without doubt the hero of my early years."

The beauty of taking inspiration from the creation of other musicians I suppose. In the same article, Hodgson was quoted; "True inspiration happens in a magical space. Many composers of classical music have not regarded themselves as creators but as mediums of the music. I can confirm that. Inspiration only happens when the mind is quiet. It is the music which directs me and not vice versa. When I'm playing it's a very similar thing. Then I do not think but let the music take me, I become one with it. It is more of a listening rather than actively doing something." I advocate that it is particularly fascinating that not only is Hodgson a brilliant musician but the way in which he is able to describe and articulate what it is that drives him as an artist is incredible; not all musicians seem as capable of doing this as eloquently. Fair play to him.

Roger Hodgson is one of those people who was probably always going to be destined to have some kind of career in music. He was quoted in *The San Diego Union Tribune* in February 2011 as he explained in detail his musical journey from a young age; "The guitar was my first instrument. My father had an old acoustic guitar that I used to drool over, but he never used to let me touch it. When my parents divorced, it was his parting gift to me. I was twelve at the time and took this guitar with me to boarding school in England. The moment I got it into my hands, my life changed forever. A teacher showed me three chords and every spare moment, even between classes, I would go and play it. Within a year, I actually did my first concert at school of all original songs. So I got the bug very, very quickly and started writing songs immediately. I took an interest in piano when I was sixteen. I was primarily self-taught and developed my own piano playing technique. I have always experimented with different sounds. My original demo for 'Dreamer', for instance, was recorded on a two-track. I was at my mother's house and did not have any percussion, so you can hear me banging boxes and lampshades on there. At seventeen, I don't know why, but I was driven to find a pump organ, which is a harmonium. It's like an organ that you play with your feet. I found one in the backroom of this old lady's house covered in cobwebs. I bought it for twenty four pounds, took it home, cleaned it up and proceeded to write many songs on it — 'Breakfast In America', 'Soapbox Opera', 'It's Raining Again', 'Two Of Us', even part of 'Fool's Overture' and 'The Logical Song'. It had that magical quality to it that helped me lose myself in the sound of the instrument. It still does; I still have it at my studio. The sound on the recording of 'Breakfast In America' is this harmonium and a grand piano combined."

Hodgson was quoted in *Goldmine* in November 2007; "I really think of myself as quite a primitive piano player, keyboard player. I did take music lessons, or piano lessons, for a year or two when I was a teenager, but they didn't really help. I never got into reading. It was more I just got into playing for fun and out of it, came a very unique style that's actually more percussive, more rhythmic and percussive, than technical. I mean, I think if a classical pianist, a good classical pianist looked at my style, he'd say, 'Oh my God, how can he play like that? Your hands are in the wrong position, etc., etc.' But it works for me, and I think it was more of a percussive, rhythmical feel that I just developed and it developed over the years. And then, obviously, I did have the very primitive 'Dreamer', the very staccato piano style, that I, you know, trademarked. I never analysed things as we went along, really. I think the older you get, then you start getting into analysing, but at the time I was just doing what came naturally, and that's what came naturally."

Roger was quoted in *New Musical Express* in August 1977; "In our own way we try to write as sincerely as possible, and that's what a lot of people pick up on. We write about things that people feel, whether it's their own private search for some meaning in life or whether it's their own private search for a woman. In the sixties there were a lot of sincere musicians singing about things that were real to them, but there's a great lack of that in the seventies."

Evidently, there was so much thought and consideration put into Supertramp's albums. As Roger Hodgson was quoted in *The San Diego Union Tribune* in February 2011; "It was very important to me back then not to create just a hit single, which most bands were focused on. I wanted to create a whole listening experience where people were taken through a range of emotions — where at the end of the album they really felt like they had been taken on a journey and had a full-course meal, if you like. I'd spend days and sometimes weeks choosing the right songs and the right order of songs, so one song flowed into the next pacing wise and emotionally. I did this for the concerts as well as the albums, and I still do this today." It's great to consider that so much care and passion went into the making of each album, regardless of how well they may or may not have been received commercially. Each one is a piece of art in its own right.

Endearingly, in the same interview, Hodgson continued, "One of the things that I like most about making music is how it has brought people together from all over the globe and how many lasting friendships have been made through a common love of my songs. It is a very special and personal connection I have with many of my fans and that the fans have with one another. I feel it's because my songs came from my deepest longing and joy and pain and touch those same places in the hearts of the people who listen. At my concerts, I'm now seeing three generations singing along with me and it's very fulfilling to see more and more young people discovering my music and it is another thing that motivates me to continue to perform."

Although Supertramp released more studio than live albums, the live shows had a unique energy about them in terms of spectacle and general energy. Sadly I am writing this as someone who was too young to see such shows but anyone who got to do that must have had a fascinating experience with it. It really comes across that a lot of thought, planning and hard work went into giving the audience something spectacular. John Helliwell was quoted in *Cash Box* in February 1988; "We view ourselves as musicians, not ego-superstars with the spotlight on them. The personalities are back a bit, so what you watch is the stage, lights and visuals which consists of a number of different films we've put together over the years. We update the films with each tour so they are a little different. We'll still have the well-known train sequence for 'Rudy'. We have a new film for the new album cut, 'An Awful Thing To Waste', which is a song about wasting talent. The real test of a group is what you do live. With help, you can make almost anything work in the studio. But live, that's different."

Although there was a strong element of spectacle to Supertramp's shows, it was very much about the music. The emphasis, from the band's perspective at least, was that they wanted to make music that people would listen to. They weren't targeting an audience who wanted to go to a concert for the sake of being rowdy. As John Helliwell was quoted in *Sounds* in May 1976; "If we're playing and somebody yells out 'Boogie!' it doesn't bother us too much, it just bothers the people around that person. It doesn't put us off really because it doesn't happen that much. We don't really get people shouting bad things. It's usually people shouting out 'Supertramp are aaall riiiight!' but then the best one was somewhere in England and we asked if everyone was listening and we stopped and there was a five second period of quietness from the audience and then somebody yelled out 'perfect' and everybody clapped."

It must have been disconcerting for the band when at one particular concert, during Davies' introduction to 'Poor Boy', a woman ran onto the stage and grabbed hold of him, almost knocking him off of his stool! As positive as the admiration must have been, it was not necessarily what Supertramp had in mind for their image. Helliwell was quoted in the same feature in *Sounds*; "I know when I go to concerts I just go to listen to the music. You just want to be able to hear everything and see everything and see the band play and really dig on the music." That said, by the time of *Breakfast In America* in 1979, the dancer in the banana costume kind of helps to throw the philosophy of "music only" out of the window a little bit. Still though, it does come across that Supertramp were, overall, musicians' musicians and not seeking to play up to a crowd as individual personalities.

Roger was quoted in *Melody Maker* in November 1975; "Polite audiences? You wouldn't have thought that if you'd been with us at Lancaster University last night. They were all upfront stamping out of time with the music. Then some idiot started screaming 'mob rule' down the microphone. I hope he wasn't a Supertramp fan. Obviously if you have a hit single it's going to attract all kinds of people."

In the same feature, Dougie Thomson was quoted as he added to Roger's point; "I don't want to see people like that in our audiences again. Fortunately we don't get them very much." Bob Siebenberg added; "We prefer people to just listen. Sometimes we've noticed in concerts that they wait until the very last note has died away before they start applauding. We really prefer to play in a theatre situation where people are seated, and have very few distractions. If you wanted to describe us in a nutshell, I guess you could simply say we're a theatre band – a group of guys who like to play in a proper concert hall atmosphere."

Hodgson was quoted in *New Musical Express* in August 1977; "We're inside a bubble and it's really hard to see what people think of us outside it. When you're back living a day to day life you can't see yourself as anything special, you're not the big superstar that everyone says you are, and I think we've been in it too long for success to change anything. We knew one day it was going to come. It's come here, it's coming to America, it's come and gone in England. Nothing's going to change us. We're still the same people. What's the point driving around in limos when we can get hire cars cheaper, it's much more functional. It's all a load of bullshit anyway. If we started letting success go to our heads, then we'd soon be a dead band and dead people... I just see how success has affected other writers, because what I write is what I am. If I stop writing then I am dead. Writers have got to be looking for something beyond success, even if it's just making greater music. I've seen a lot of my idols from the sixties stop writing any worthwhile music. They get the money coming in, they get women, they get the drugs flowing through the door, they get their mansion and they get their own really comfortable scene. Their minds are so preoccupied with all the daily comforts of living that there's nothing to write about. They divorce themselves from the real world if you like."

As journalist Tony Stewart reported in the same feature in *New Musical Express*; "Since their first success this group have rarely presented a strikingly interesting public image. They approached interviews with indifference, and their reluctance to divulge anything about themselves or their music has always seemed illustrative of either disdain for the mechanics of the rock business or thickness. Most people believed it was the latter." Thickness as in an intellectual lack of substance or thickness in terms of putting a wall up to journalists? I'm not entirely sure what Stewart meant here to be honest but either way, the point remains that there was certainly a considerable extent of discretion with which Supertramp presented in the public eye. In the same interview though, Rick and Roger seemed candid about some of their experiences regarding how the public had responded to them. Roger was quoted; "You've got to shape up or ship out. You're doing live radios every day so you get to know what you're all about. We've had an unbelievable number of people come up and say incredible things – like we've changed their lives or whatever. When we were in Britain, a Canadian guy who was just about to commit suicide phoned our manager. He said, 'Put me on to Rick and Rog, they're the only ones who know anything in this world. They're the only ones who can save me'." The duo didn't take the call but their manager patiently and kindly did. Davies was quoted; "I've had quite a few people come up to me lately to say that we've saved their marriage. It makes you think you're doing something worthwhile. It really is helping people." For a band who didn't want to engage with the whole celebrity and rock star thing, Supertramp certainly made their mark.

Olympia, Paris, 5th October 2012.

Roger Hodgson during a private concert at Reithalle Hessstrasse in Munich, 8th October 2012.

John Helliwell attending IWC Race Night Dinner in Geneva, Switzerland, 22nd January 2013. The swiss watch manufacturer celebrated its new Ingenieur collection as well as the partnership with the Mercedes AMG Petronas Formula One Team.

Roger at the Press conference for
'Night of the Proms 2017' at Hotel
Gastwerk in Hamburg,
2nd December 2017.

Roger Hodgson at the Monte Carlo Sporting Summer Festival on 10th August 2017.

© Syspeo / Andia / Alamy Stock Photo

Roger Hodgson at Las Noches del Botanico
Festival at the Real Jardín Botánico, Madrid,
24th July 2019.

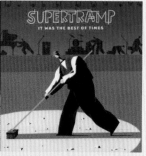

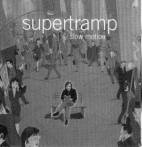

Full Discography (Including solo releases)

Supertramp (1970)
Indelibly Stamped (1971)
Crime Of The Century (1974)
Crisis? What Crisis? (1975)
Even In The Quietest Moments... (1977)
Breakfast In America (1979)
Paris (1980)
...Famous Last Words... (1982)
Brother Where You Bound (1985)
The Autobiography Of Supertramp (1986)
Free As A Bird (1987)
Live '88 (1988)
The Very Best Of Supertramp (1990)
The Very Best Of Supertramp 2 (1992)
Some Things Never Change (1997)
It Was The Best Of Times (1999)
Is Everybody Listening? (2001)
Slow Motion (2002)
Retrospectacle – The Supertramp Anthology (2005)
70-10 Tour (2010)

Supertramp was listed among hundreds of artists whose material was reportedly destroyed in the 2008 fire at Universal Studios in *The New York Times Magazine* in June 2019. However, the scale of the damage caused by the fire was such that a) this information is not a dead cert and b) if material did get destroyed, there is no specific information available as to what it was.

Roger Hodgson albums

In The Eye Of The Storm (1984)
Hai Hai (1987)
Rites Of Passage (1997)
Open The Door (2000)
Classics Live (2010)

Bob Siebenberg albums

Giants In Our Own Room (1986)
Glendale River (2013)

John Helliwell enjoying the Oktoberfest in Munich, 28th September 2019

© Felix Hörhager/dpa/Alamy Live News

About The Author

Laura Shenton MA LLCM DipRSL has been thinking about music since she first heard it, possibly whilst still in the womb. She has a Masters degree in "Music Since 1900" from Liverpool Hope University. Her hobbies and interests include writing, playing the piano, staying up into the small hours wondering about life whilst eating crisps and obsessing about music, hamsters and dogs. In particular, her writing buddy is the best dog in the world — a black Labrador.